TEMPLE ISRAEL of Greater Miami

Synagogue
in the Central City:

TEMPLE ISRAEL
of Greater Miami
1922-1972

Charlton W. Tebeau

University of Miami Press
Coral Gables, Florida

Designed by Bernard Lipsky

Manufactured in the United States of America

Illustration credits: Mrs. Morris Graff, p. 149. Mrs. Isaac Levin, p. 60. Sie Mendelson, p. 57. *The Miami News,* p. 33. Monroe County Public Library, Key West, p. 31. Romer Collection, Miami Public Library, pp. 21, 27, 40, 63. State Photographic Archives, pp. 23, 24, 42. Temple Israel Archives, pp. 61, 64, 70, 72, 78, 80, 82, 83, 85, 87, 91, 100, 102, 106, 111, 112, 127, 128, 130, 136, 141, 146, 154, 155. University of Miami Library, p. 88. C. H. Ward, *Lure of the Southland,* p. 38. Mrs. Sydney L. Weintraub, p. 35. H. Franklin Williams, pp. 93, 132. Mitchell Wolfson, p. 29. Myron Zeientz, p. 74. Colman Zwitman family, pp. 96, 97.

The Sisterhood, as part of its contribution
to the golden anniversary celebration,
has underwritten the cost of writing this book.

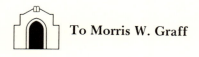 **To Morris W. Graff**

Contents

Illustrations

Foreword

The children of Israel in Miami were few in number, but they built a sanctuary and dedicated it to their God. They prayed in their own way, taught their children as they themselves believed, and established their faith with courage and with conviction. From time to time new leaders—both lay and spiritual—rose to guide and to inspire them. In song, in spoken word, and in meditation, the message of Torah, the utterance of prophets, and the teachings of the wise and the reverent resounded through the halls of their sanctuary. In keeping with ancestral heritage the purpose of their thrice-blessed house was abundantly fulfilled in prayer, in study, and in assembly.

The years passed, and neither the leaders nor the people —who increased in numbers—were content to have their sanctuary remain a mere shrine. They worshiped God and then went out to translate their renewed faith into daily living. They sat at the feet of teachers and remembered that "not the word but the deed is the essence of the matter." And, after meeting in friendship and in mutual concern, each departed to his own arena of service in the larger secular life of which he was a part.

The laughter of children, the new sounds of youths, the

hopes of brides and grooms, the sighs of those in the autumn of their lives, and the weeping of the bereaved—all these sounds and more were heard within the walls of this house of Israel. Here, too, there echoed and left a mark in the hearts of many the agonies of a world in travail—the thunder of wars, the cry of the innocent martyrs, the triumphant sounds of a Jerusalem reborn.

In a new era, these children of Israel looked into a tomorrow laden with both promise and fear. Before them was the promise of progress, of knowledge, of achievement. But before them, also, was the terror of violence, of deprivation, of destruction. Like the ancient seer, these people asked, "Watchman, what of the night?" And with the same faith that moved Isaiah, they knew they had but one answer: "The morning cometh, but also the night." God's plan of orderliness and oneness for the universe would prevail, at last, over the chaos and divisiveness which man had wrought.

After five decades, these children of Israel paused to express their gratitude to God, thanking Him for keeping them alive, sustaining them, and bringing them to this hour. They stopped to remember those who had died and to whom much was owed. They stayed to express their appreciation to those still blessed with life. In celebration they honored the pioneers, the builders, and the founders. And, finally, they resolved to record the history of their house of prayer—which had become a house of prayer for all people—so that other generations might know and, hopefully, look back from time to time in thanks.

Joseph R. Narot

Preface

This book was planned to mark the golden anniversary of Miami's first Reform Jewish congregation. The committee planning the observance recognized that to make the history a meaningful account of those fifty years involved more than recounting the internal affairs of the Temple Israel congregation. The religious heritage of the members and the way they interpret it are, of course, basic to the story. The work of the lay and spiritual leadership and of the auxiliary organizations within the group is no less important. But these factors cannot give us the complete picture because the congregation is also part of the larger secular community in which its members live. The number and the relative importance of the membership in that community are also significant measures of the role of the Temple.

With these considerations in mind the committee decided to select a professional historian outside the congregation with interest and experience in the study and writing of local history to write the book. As it turned out, the committee's choice was also outside the Jewish faith, a fact which necessitated that I learn something of Judaism in general and Reform Judaism in particular.

If the book is less than a full account of all the internal affairs of the congregation, it is also far more than that. It aims to tell of the people and the circumstances that created, shaped, and directed the Temple and of the role that it and its members have played in the community. If the names of all the leading figures are not mentioned, we should remember that in the history of such a congregational effort there will be many unsung heroes whose contributions, although unidentified, have been no less essential to the life of the Temple.

The story begins with an account of the development of the Greater Miami community to about 1922 when the congregation was organized. The second chapter describes the early Jewish community out of which the congregation came. The third chapter continues the background with a descriptive historical discussion of the place of Reform Judaism in Jewish religion.

Temple Israel originated in 1922 in a tourist-oriented community already taking on metropolitan characteristics. The Temple was launched in a very small Jewish community on the eve of a land boom that grew to fantastic proportions and from which the Temple was both beneficiary and victim. The Florida depression began in 1926, accented by a September hurricane that buried any hope that the boom could be revived. The national depression began with the stock market crash in October of 1929, and before recovery had been accomplished the second World War intervened. Only after a quarter of a century of struggle that achieved little more than survival did the congregation recover some of the optimism of its founders and begin to realize some of their early hopes and promise. Then growth became so rapid as to be almost overwhelming. The problems of success in the inflationary second half of the first fifty years were as vexing in their ways as those of the deflationary first half.

The sources of information for this account are mostly congregational. The minutes of meetings of the Temple Board of Trustees, the congregation, and the auxiliary groups provided the basic data. Oral history, some of it recorded on tape, transcribed, and placed in the archives of the Temple, adds a strong personal element.

Interviews with the following twenty-four persons were taped and transcribed: Leo Ackerman, Elliott D. Blumenthal, Jacob Bornstein, Edward Cohen, Audrey Finkelstein, Richard Gerstein, Sam Goldstein, Morris W. Graff, Mrs. Herman I. Homa, Steven Jacobs, William Lehman, Sam C. Levenson, Belle (Mrs. Isaac) Levin, Baron de Hirsh Meyer, Joseph R. Narot, Max Orovitz, Jules Pearlman, Nat Roth, Dorothy (Mrs. Maurice) Serotta, William D. Singer, Harold Thurman, Claire (Mrs. Sydney L.) Weintraub, Henry C. Wolff, and Mitchell Wolfson. Mrs. Weintraub also made available the very important papers left by her father, Isidor Cohen.

The Temple Israel *Bulletin,* published weekly since 1939 except during the summer months, provided a week-by-week schedule of events. Discussions with individuals provided both information and insight. The extracongregational sources are principally the newspapers in the community, particularly *The Miami News,* formerly *The Miami Metropolis,* founded in 1896, *The Miami Herald* and its antecedent *The Miami Evening Record,* which first appeared on September 15, 1903, and *The Jewish Floridian,* published from 1927 to 1939 by J. Louis Shochet and after his death in 1939 by Shochet's son, Fred.

To a great degree in writing this book I have been the coordinator of the efforts of many people. I assume responsibility for the final form of the narrative and for the judgment as to who and what should be included. Although I cannot mention everyone who has helped in developing the material and in preparing the manuscript, I must in all honesty recognize some of them. First is the late Morris W. Graff, who served the congregation as assistant rabbi from 1957 until his retirement in June 1971. He looked forward to spending his first retired months on this project. The book lacks something because of his death in the following August, and appropriately the book is dedicated to him.

Interviews with large numbers of persons have been most helpful. Among those persons deserving special mention are

Cantor Jacob Bornstein, Mrs. Joseph Bulbin, Alvin M. Cassel, Mrs. Reba Engler Daner, Mrs. Rose Davis, Mrs. Lenore Fleming and her son, Joseph, Mrs. Carol Goldman, Mrs. Ruth Graff, Mr. and Mrs. Aaron Kanner, Mr. and Mrs. Maurice Kohen, J. Gerald Lewis, Seymour Liebman, Mr. and Mrs. Sie Mendelson, Mrs. Howard Novell, Mr. and Mrs. Nat Roth, Mrs. Maurice Serotta, Mrs. Harold Spaet, Mrs. I. M. Weinstein, Mrs. Claire Weintraub, Mrs. Isaac Wolkowsky, and George Wolpert. Key West background was generously supplied by Mrs. Betty M. Bruce of the Monroe County Public Library, Mr. and Mrs. Halbert Lewinsky, Joe Pearlman, David Wolkowsky, and Rabbi Nathan Zwitman of Temple B'nai Zion, all of Key West.

The manuscript has been read, all or in part, by Dr. Sidney L. Besvinick, Mr. Edward Cohen, Dr. Joseph R. Narot, and Dr. Julian I. Weinkle, all of whom have made valuable suggestions and have saved me from error. Mr. Adon Taft, religion editor of *The Miami Herald,* has been helpful with suggestions and materials. Marcia (Mrs. Lewis) Kanner became a full partner in the enterprise about half way through the preparation of the manuscript. She developed the material for the chapters on the religious school and the Sisterhood. The members of the Temple staff have been cordial and helpful; deserving special mention are Mrs. Mildred Benis, secretary to Rabbi Narot; Mrs. Nettie Werner, secretary and executive assistant to the Temple administrator; and Mrs. Beatrice Muskat, Temple librarian, whose sanctum was our base of operations.

Charlton W. Tebeau
Coral Gables, Florida

TEMPLE
ISRAEL
of Greater
Miami

1/Miami, Florida:
From Frontier
to Budding Metropolis

Anyone who sees metropolitan Miami for the first time today finds it difficult, if not impossible, to realize how close to raw frontier the area was in 1922 when the first steps were being taken to organize Temple Israel. Florida had been a part of the United States for a century but had barely begun to come into its own. The United States census in 1920 counted just under a million (968,470) people in the state. Dade County, which was little more than Greater Miami, had been created by act of the Legislative Council in 1836 but in 1920 counted only 42,753 residents, 29,571 of them, almost 70 percent, in Miami. And for all the spectacular development in Miami Beach during the previous decade, it reported only 644. Not until 1940 did Florida, the twenty-seventh state to enter the American Union, reach that rank in population among the states. Then came the population explosion that placed Florida twentieth in 1950, tenth in 1960, and ninth in 1965, with a population in 1970 of 6,815,702. More importantly for our purpose, 1,263,540 persons, about the same number as were in the entire state as recently as 1925 at the height of the booming twenties and one-fifth of the total in 1970, lived in Dade County. With adjoining

Broward County now second only to Dade in population and Palm Beach County fifth, the three together account for a third of the state's population. Temple Israel expanded along with this explosive growth and experienced many of the same growing pains.

Very likely there was not a white resident in the Miami area in 1821 at the time of the change of flags. There may not even have been an Indian here. The aboriginal Tequesta Indians, once numbering an estimated 800, had all been gone since 1763 when a small remnant of them left with the departing Spaniards. The Seminoles, comparative newcomers to Florida, visited the region only on seasonal hunting expeditions. The strategic location of land on Biscayne Bay had been recognized by some early explorers. Land grants in the British era of 1763-1784 and the succeeding Second Spanish occupation preempted large tracts in what is now downtown Miami, north and south of the Miami River, but these tracts were not settled.

Nor were there any settlers at Key West. The entire island had been granted to Juan P. Salas in 1818, but development did not begin until the American period. During this period, because of its strategic location on the sailing route between the Gulf of Mexico and the Caribbean and the Atlantic and its deep channels and protected harbor, Key West became for a time in the second half of the nineteenth century the largest city in Florida. Ships from around the world stopped there and made it one of the most cosmopolitan New World cities. The railroad age that rescued Miami from isolation and obscurity left Key West outside the mainstream of American economic activity. Among the Key Westers who moved to Miami were some of the founders of Temple Israel.

At the end of the American Revolution many of the loyalist British subjects who had left Florida and other southeastern English colonies established new homes in the islands of the British West Indies. They visited the Florida Keys and the mainland to hunt, to fish, to cut timber, to collect sea turtles and their eggs, and to engage in marine salvage, or "wrecking" as it was popularly known, along the Florida Reef. However, these

Conchs, as they came to be known, did not immediately settle in Florida.

Much seaborne traffic passed by Miami in sight of the outer beaches. Since the days of the Spanish treasure fleets the Gulf Stream northward to Cape Canaveral had been an important sea-lane. Ships came into Biscayne Bay only to escape bad weather or to get freshwater. One of the first actions of the U.S. government in the newly acquired area was to establish a naval station at Key West to eliminate piracy in the nearby Caribbean waters. At about the same time, in 1825, the Cape Florida Lighthouse and its light began to guide mariners along the treacherous Florida Reef. But this traffic was offshore, and there was as yet no idea that behind that fringe of islands lay an area that one day would experience spectacular development and become the home of one of the largest Jewish communities in the United States. In fact, so desolate, unoccupied, and isolated was the southeast coast that the U.S. government established four houses of refuge along the coast in the 1870s. The southernmost house was located on Miami Beach where, though deactivated earlier, it stood until 1926. At these stations stranded victims of wrecks who had made it to shore could find

Cape Florida lighthouse and keeper's living quarters, the oldest permanent structure built by the white man in Dade County. Operated from 1825 to 1878 except for interruptions during the Seminole and U.S. Civil wars, it is now in Cape Florida State Park.

food, water, and shelter. The "barefoot mailman" and others who in the absence of roads walked the beach sand also used them for rest stations. Keepers of lighthouses and refuge stations were among the first settlers along the southeast coast.

Dade County originated in 1836 and at this time included the area that has become Palm Beach and Broward counties. Dade County received its name from an event that occurred far away in Florida at the time of its creation. Major Francis L. Dade was leading 111 men from Fort Brooke on Tampa Bay to Fort King near present-day Ocala. On December 28, 1835, when the worst part of the journey seemed over, they walked into an ambush in which Dade and all but three of his men died.

Miami did not at first become the county seat; that distinction went to Indian Key, seventy-five miles southwest of Miami, just off what is now the Overseas Highway. Sea channels at Indian Key were deep enough for small ships to come in close to shore, making the key accessible to seagoing trade. Also, Indian Key lay near the Florida Reef where the business of "wrecking" flourished, and it was far enough from the watchful eye of the U.S. District Court at Key West, which administered marine salvage, to attract those persons who profited from operating on the outer limits if not outside the law. Enterprising merchants also did some trading with Indians and settlers scattered along the Keys.

All this came to a cataclysmic end early on August 7, 1840, when seventeen canoeloads of Seminole Indians raided the island. They killed Dr. Henry Perrine, who was staying there temporarily until Indian danger subsided and he could get to work at plant introduction on the mainland. Six others also lost their lives. The Seminoles looted and burned the principal store and warehouse and other buildings. Indian Key never recovered. The county seat was moved to Miami in 1844, but the Miami area did not grow in importance. In an election in 1888 a majority of the Dade County voters approved moving the county seat to Juno at the north end of Lake Worth; however, the prestige of Juno was short-lived. The "Celestial Railroad" from Juno to Jupiter, with Mars and Venus in between, was absorbed by the

Florida East Coast Railroad. Indian River steamboat traffic was no longer important. As soon as the required ten-year waiting period elapsed, a new election returned the county seat to Miami.

The year 1896 was the magic one for which Miami had been waiting. Henry Morrison Flagler's Florida East Coast Railroad reached the community on April 15, thereby ending Miami's isolation. Miami no longer played second fiddle to Coconut Grove and Lemon City but became the population, business, and governmental center of the Biscayne Bay region. The city received its charter on July 26 that year, and *The Miami Metropolis,* now *The Miami News,* the community's first newspaper, began publication. That year also witnessed the first observance of the Jewish High Holy Days in Miami.

The Miami Metropolis in its first issue described the community. Miami had one bank, three physicians, one dentist, two law offices, three restaurants, two druggists, one lumber company, one cigar manufacturer, one hotel, two pool rooms, a number of taverns (north of the city limits), two real estate offices, one livery business, and twelve retail establishments. Isidor Cohen, the principal figure in the early Jewish community, wrote in the paper at the end of the year: "We have a city hall, a jail, a volunteer fire department, water and light systems. . . . " Also by the end of the year sixteen retail clothing

Automobiles parked at Smith's Casino, Miami Beach, at the end of Collins Bridge, 1922

stores were established; only four of their owners were not Jewish.

Growth did not become rapid until the second decade of the new century. One measure of the new growth was the division of the upper half of huge Dade County into Palm Beach County in 1909 and Broward County in 1915. Perhaps the greatest new stimulus for expansion was the Everglades drainage program inaugurated in the years of the Napoleon B. Broward governorship, 1905-1909. This creation of more solid land spawned a speculative real estate boom of immense proportions all along the eastern side of the Glades. The new land together with the increasing tempo of life on Miami Beach, which had received its charter in 1913, did much to advertise the region and bring prospectors, many of whom remained to become investors and permanent residents. William Jennings Bryan began trading in Dade County real estate and built his home "Villa Serena." He left Miami in early 1913 to become secretary of state in the cabinet of President Woodrow Wilson. Later he broke with the president and returned to live in Miami until his death in 1925.

Airview of Miami Beach, 1920

In 1912 the first train reached Key West over the Florida East Coast Railway Company's extension to the island. The hopes of the builders were never realized but trains continued to operate on the line until 1935 when the Labor Day hurricane destroyed much of the track, bridges, causeways, and rolling stock. The management decided to abandon the railroad south of Florida City. The Florida Highway Department acquired the property and constructed on the right-of-way the present Overseas Highway to Key West. In 1915 construction started on the Tamiami Trail westward from Miami across the Everglades and up the west coast to Tampa. Although not completed until 1928, this route continued to promise new access. More important, the completion and continuing improvement of the highway northward to Jacksonville and beyond began to bring additional visitors and prospectors, a necessary ingredient in the land boom getting under way in the early and middle twenties.

The United States became involved in two wars during Miami's early history. The War for Cuban Independence, April 24 to August 12, 1898, came conveniently between winter seasons. Only lack of a deep harbor prevented the city from capitalizing on the services of the railroad as Tampa was able to do. Miamians feared attack and organized volunteer home guard units in the city and in Coconut Grove. Largely through the influence of railroad officials, Miami finally got a training camp, but the presence of 7,000 men from June 24 to August 13 was so overwhelming that Miamians were as pleased as the soldiers when they were pulled out.

The First World War, which the United States entered in April 1917, was a more serious matter. Although actual combat was an ocean away, Miamians went off to war and never returned. The "flu" epidemic in 1918 and 1919 was in its way as disruptive as yellow fever had been in earlier times.

Yellow fever was the most dreaded menace to health until the cause was discovered at the end of the nineteenth century and the disease was quickly eliminated. Fortunately no outbreaks occurred in the army camps during the war. Lack of camp sanitation did result in a very high incidence of typhoid fever which gave rise to reports that water in Florida's cities was contaminated. (A yellow fever epidemic, the last the city was to experience, had occurred in 1899. The city was under quarantine from mid-September to mid-December, but it did not materially affect the growth of the area.) Even though the war stimulated food production, wartime shortages of manpower and materials, coupled with rising prices and wages, sharply curtailed some aspects of business development, but not for long because the war ended in November 1918.

This increasing tempo of economic development did not by any means remove the evidences of Miami's frontier and rural origin. But urban problems that have a modern ring were beginning to appear. In 1917 the city's board of health reported the need for more garbage cans and more mules. A year later the city was preparing to charge householders three dollars a year for the garbage cans the city had been supplying. In 1922 the Civitan Club suggested that the garbage should be collected more than once a week. The mules were also beginning to constitute a problem. The demand was growing for the city and for private owners to move their stables and barns beyond the city limits. In 1911 Howard Gill exhibited the first airplane, and in October 1922 the City Commission created an Aviation Advisory Board. Especially indicative of the contrast between the old and the new in the city was the notice in the summer of 1918 that City Attorney F. M. Hudson was drafting an ordinance to bar roosters in the central city "especially near hotels and others places where tourists are liable to locate in great numbers . . . especially those who need rest at night."

Miamians were well on the way to establishing themselves as a churchgoing people, a fact often obscured by Miami's image as a recreation area affording entertainment for tourists. Another interesting feature was the astounding variety of organizations at such an early date. A church directory in one of the daily newspapers in May 1922 lists the churches: one Adventist, six Baptist, one Catholic, two Christian Science, one Christian, one Church of Christ, one Church of God, four Congregational, one Free Methodist, three Lutheran, three Episcopal, four Methodist Episcopal, six Methodist, one Nazarene, two Pentecostal, one Presbyterian, one Southern Presbyterian, one Salvation Army, three Spiritualist, one Theosophy, and one Universalist. Also listed were an International Bible Students Association, a Christian Missionary Alliance, and a New Thought Centre. Any reference to Temple Beth David appeared on Fridays. It was the only synagogue in the city.

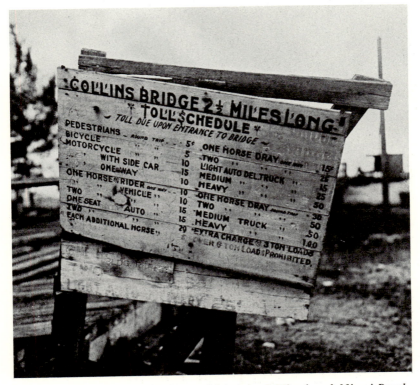

Toll schedule for Collins Bridge, which joined Miami and Miami Beach, 1924. The bridge was opened in 1912 and closed in 1925 to be replaced by the Venetian Causeway.

Frontier to Budding Metropolis [27]

2/The Miami
Jewish Community,
1896-1922

It should occasion no surprise that there were Jews in Miami in its frontier days. There had been Jews on earlier Florida frontiers. A few lived in Pensacola and Saint Augustine as early as the British period. One of the most prominent Florida pioneers at the beginning of the American period in 1821 was Moses Elias Levy. He had migrated from Morocco in North Africa to the Virgin Islands and then to Cuba. In the last days of the Spanish era in Florida he acquired an extensive land grant in present-day Alachua County. He planned to establish a colony of Orthodox Jews on the land, perhaps to make an American refuge for them. He secured U.S. citizenship for himself and his family at the time of the change of flags, and the United States recognized the validity of his land claims. His son David served as territorial delegate to the Congress of the United States and participated in the convention that drafted Florida's first state constitution. David Levy was a principal promoter of statehood, which was achieved in 1845, and he became one of Florida's first two U.S. senators, the first Jew to sit in that body. In the same year his name became David Levy Yulee by act of the state legislature. He became a major producer of sugar on a plantation near

Homosassa and went on to organize the company that built Florida's first cross-state railroad, from Fernandina to Cedar Key. The family went somewhat into eclipse after his death shortly after the war.

The spectacular success of the Yulee family was not accompanied by any considerable migration of Jews to the new state. The first Jewish cemetery in Jacksonville was not established until 1854. There were, however, enough Jews in Jacksonville and Pensacola by the time of the U.S. Civil War, 1861-65, to meet in private homes for religious services. In 1884 *The American Israelite* of Cincinnati could find in the peninsular part of the state only one couple in Tampa and a family at Fort Meade. Tampa, like Miami, did not begin to grow until the railroad reached the port city in 1884. Ten years later in October the city's Jews organized congregation Shaari Zedek, which received its charter in December.

At much the same time a considerable Jewish population was growing at Key West, then the largest city in Florida. Mitchell Wolfson reports that his father's brother Joe landed there by chance in 1884 when his ship was wrecked on the Florida Reef. He liked the place well enough to induce his brother Louis and

Louis Wolfson's store in Key West, 1904. The store was later razed to make way for La Concha Hotel.

his family to join him. Others soon followed them. Practically all the Jews in Key West became peddlers, giving the city's merchants so much competition that the city commission placed a $1,000 fee on licenses for peddlers. This fee forced the Jews to become merchants; most of them went into dry goods and clothing, but some went into groceries and furniture. They were soon accepted as indicated by Louis Wolfson becoming a member of the city commission. His son Mitchell became the first Jewish mayor of Miami Beach in 1940-1942, which was before the city became known as a Jewish stronghold. Baron de Hirsch Meyer had earlier become a member of the city commission. It is easily overlooked that "the Beach" was developed by Gentiles. Louis Wolfson's grandson, Mitchell's son Louis II, currently represents Dade County in the state legislature. Another Key Wester, Abe Aronovitz, who came to Miami in 1922 and was associated with Temple Israel from the beginning, became mayor of Miami in 1950.

In the early days of Greater Miami anti-Jewish practices were present, notably on Miami Beach. Most Jews who experienced the treatment insist that it was not directed against them as individuals but that it was for business reasons. Miami Beach was at first almost exclusively developed by Gentiles, and the sales appeal was primarily to them. Mitchell Wolfson recalls that the Anti-Defamation League commissioned him to take the issue to Miami's two daily newspapers shortly after the Knight family took over publishing *The Miami Herald.* The papers had been accepting advertising of restricted sales, but after Wolfson's plea both papers accepted the principle involved and ceased publishing advertisements for restricted property and facilities. Wolfson cited his own experience later as a city councilman and mayor of Miami Beach as proof of his contention that discrimination was not a personal matter. Rabbi Narot and other spokesmen for the Temple have continued to call attention to all forms of ethnic discrimination, specifically to instances where Jews are excluded from participation. Although there has been no extensive violence and no confrontation, anti-Semitism, both latent and overt, does exist in the Greater Miami area, and the Jewish community is alert to it, preferring usually to fight it on the broad front of human dignity, equality, and justice rather than as a separate issue.

In 1896 when the first Jews were moving into the infant city of Miami, the Key West Jews were organizing a congregation they named Rodef Sholem. At first they met on the second floor of Louis Fine's furniture store. In 1905 they purchased what had been the home of Dr. John B. Maloney and converted it into a synagogue, possibly the only one in the United States with a widow's walk on top. In the same year Rabbi Julian Shapo became their spiritual leader. For a time they split into two groups, the second taking the name of B'nai Zion. They soon reconciled their differences, however, and Conservative B'nai Zion has since been the only congregation in Key West.

When the Florida East Coast Railroad began to be pushed southward in the latter part of the nineteenth century, enterprising businessmen, some of them Jewish, followed its progress southward. They set up offices and shops at each new terminus that seemed to promise economic rewards, especially at Titusville, Fort Pierce, and West Palm Beach. Few of them remained in the new places very long; they either abandoned the hope of an eldorado at the end of the railroad and returned northward or extended their search to other new places. The middle nineties were depression years, and Americans, immigrant and native-born alike, ranged far and wide in search of

Key West synagogue
with a widow's walk on top

opportunity. The railroad age was opening up Florida as it had many other areas of the United States.

The railroad brought Miami its first Jews of record, and some of them remained to play prominent roles in the life of the community. Who came first is not entirely clear. Joseph Schneidman may have been the first to come to the area, but he stopped in Lemon City for a time before joining the growing community at the mouth of the Miami River. He came ahead of the railroad, and Lemon City had the only dock on water deep enough for coastal vessels to use. Schneidman, only five years out of Russia, had been in the haberdashery business in West Palm Beach.

Certainly the first Jew to settle and remain in Miami was Isidor Cohen. Born in Russia in 1870, he came to New York in 1883, where he attended public school. In 1891 he moved to Savannah, Georgia, where he clerked in his brother's dry goods store for awhile. He then tried his fortune briefly in several Florida towns—Titusville, Fort Pierce, Cocoa, Bartow, and Palm Beach.

Two freezes in the 1894-95 winter killed all the crops and fruit trees in east Florida and brought business to a standstill. The freeze had not reached Miami, and the railroad was on the way to getting there so Miami looked promising. Isidor Cohen packed up his stock of goods and reached Miami on February 6, ahead of the railroad. (The first train did not enter the city until April 15.) He too landed at Lemon City and transferred his boxes to a smaller boat to complete the journey. Cohen set up shop briefly on the south side of the river, but he soon moved to the north side. Thereafter, except for three years "in exile" in Jacksonville, which is discussed later, he played a prominent role in the business, civic, and religious life of the community until his death in 1951. What is more important for this history, he wrote frequently for the local newspapers on the Jewish community and in 1925 published an account of the city's history in a book, *Historical Sketches and Sidelights of Miami, Florida.*

In *The Miami Metropolis* of March 31, 1923, Cohen recalled

Isidor Cohen's store in the very early 1900s. Cohen and a saleslady are pictured in the doorway, and a customer is outside.

that, including children, there were twenty-five Jews in Miami when the railroad reached the city. Only four of the sixteen merchants in the city by the end of 1896 were not Jewish. Identifiable by name late in 1896 and early 1897 were Samuel and David Singer, Morris Kanner, Charles Kanner and family, M. Seligman and family, W. Wolfe and family, Mr. and Mrs. M. Hanes, M. Budholtz and two sons, Abe and Louis, A. Safranek and family, Miss Rebecca Siegle, and Julius M. Frank and family (wife and six children). Seven of the merchants were arrested on December 21 for keeping their stores open on Sunday. They admitted they had remained open, but their justification was not accepted, and they paid fines of one dollar and court costs. This was not a case of community hostility; *The Miami Metropolis* came to their defense.

Characteristically, Jewish merchants closed their businesses and observed the High Holy Days that first year as they have every year since. They also came together on September 11 and effected an organization with David Singer as president and Budholtz as secretary-treasurer. The next year Rabbi Aaron Hemmerman of West Palm Beach officiated at High Holy Days services. How the rabbi happened to be there and available is not recorded. More often than not in the early days a rabbi was not present and laymen conducted the services.

Disaster struck the young Miami business community on December 25, 1896, when fire burned almost all of it. The heat from the fire caused a cylinder of gas in the bottling works to explode, and flying metal killed Julius Frank in his store next door. His widow took him to Augusta, Georgia, for burial and later moved with her children to Ocala, Florida. Three of the dozen Jewish merchants left town after the fire: of the ones who remained, some relocated and some rebuilt on the same sites. Thereafter the Jewish population declined for a time. Cohen reported seven families in 1898, and only three in 1899. Among those who remained were Cohen and Schneidman, who became partners although each had a store. On September 1, 1903, Schneidman died of cancer, and Cohen purchased his half of the business and brought his own brother, Harry, to assist him in running it. The next August when Cohen went north, ostensibly on a buying trip, he married Mrs. Schneidman, who was the former Ida Herkowitz, and adopted her son, Murray. Two children, Claire (now Mrs. Sydney Weintraub) and Edward, who died in 1961, were born to the Cohens. The role the family was to play in Miami was by no means limited to work in the Jewish community. Mrs. Cohen died in 1971 at the age of 93.

On February 23, 1900, the local businessmen organized the Miami Board of Trade with nearly fifty men enrolled at the first meeting. In the same year some, if not all, of the local merchants met informally and agreed upon regular closing hours. By the summer of 1902, a loosely organized Miami Merchants Association was holding regular meetings at the stores of Cohen and Schneidman with fourteen firms represented. In 1903 in a more formal organization Cohen became president and John H. Burdine became secretary. Cohen was also active in the Board

Isidor Cohen and his family: Mrs. Cohen and the children, Claire (Mrs. Sydney L. Weintraub), Murray, and Eddie

of Trade, in which he served as treasurer in 1907. The two organizations merged in 1913 to become the Miami Chamber of Commerce, and Cohen was its first secretary.

Among the Chamber's principal concerns was the effort to get the Miami harbor deepened and improved. Like all east coast towns, Miami lacked a good natural harbor and had to wait for the dredging of an artificial channel and basin. Businessmen also hoped that waterborne freight and possibly a second railroad would end their dependence upon the services of the Florida East Coast Railroad. Isidor Cohen was among the antirailroad group that argued the carrier was abusing the monopoly it enjoyed. This was a common experience of Americans; they placed great expectations upon the coming of railroads only to discover that the costs of services ate deeply into their anticipated profits.

Cohen once said he had joined everything in Miami but the

Tuxedo Club from which only his lack of a tuxedo excluded him. In his first year in Miami he assembled with others over a hardware store to organize a Masonic Lodge, which received its charter on January 1, 1898. He was a charter member of a Benevolent Protective Order of Elks (BPOE) Lodge in 1905. He tried for elective office only once when along with ten others he offered himself for alderman. A quotation in an Orlando newspaper that seemed to place him on the side of the railroad interests perhaps contributed to his defeat. His denial and explanations availed him nothing; he ran a poor tenth. He did serve later on a charter board for city manager government and on the state Democratic Executive Committee. Cohen sold his store in 1911 to John T. Knight, the former superintendent of the Drake Lumber Company and for three years postmaster at Princeton, Florida. The next year he opened a store in Jacksonville but did not give up his roots in Miami. In 1913 he sent a check to the committee planning a Miami birthday celebration; he returned to Miami a year later and thereafter was engaged in the real estate business. He had never sold his Miami home.

In the second decade of the century the Jewish population began to grow. In 1910 Cohen estimated there were five Jewish merchants and eight or ten in other occupations. In 1915 Miami had ten Jewish families and ten unmarried adults. By 1923 this number had grown to 150 families or about 600 individuals. The state census in 1915 counted 15,437 residents and a city directory in 1923 named 51,000. In 1915 there were scarcely a hundred visiting Jews whereas in 1923 the number had possibly reached 2,000.

Isidor Cohen thought the Jewish population grew slowly until 1915 because of the lack of the institutions of communal life which made observing rituals difficult for a small group. He noted that in 1907 when his son was born he had brought Rabbi Julian Shapo from Key West for the rite of circumcision, but the minyan of ten men over thirteen years of age to serve as witnesses was made up partly of prominent non-Jews in the community. In 1915, *The Miami Metropolis,* in a survey of religious life of the community, reported a move among the forty-five to fifty Jews, many of whom were prominent businessmen, to strengthen their organization and erect a synagogue. A letter in January 1918 reported, "The two weeks I have spent here brought me into contact with a small but to all appearances rapidly growing congregation which is every winter season increased by a considerable number of transients who remain in town for 3-5 months. . . . They have a chartered congregation, possess a cemetery (since 1912) and have bought a lot for a synagogue." Cohen reported in 1923 that they had a temple, a rabbi, a shohet or ritual slaughterer, a mohel to perform the Abrahamic convenant, and a Hebrew School.

Piecing together the story of an individual is difficult, except for an occasional highly visible figure like Isidor Cohen. An interesting case in point is that of Philip A. Ullendorff, an important organizer and benefactor of Temple Israel, as well as of Miami's first congregation, Temple Beth David. In return for his generous financial support he was given the privilege of naming the new congregation when the Reform Jews left Temple Beth David. He chose Israel because it was also his father's name. Because he died one year after Temple Israel was organized, his name tends to disappear from the record and from the recollections of Temple founders still alive fifty years later. They all recall that he was a butcher and was considered wealthy. Actually, his name appeared frequently in the business and occasionally in the religious news of the community. There are also frequent references to him in the papers of Isidor Cohen.

Philip A. Ullendorff was born in Germany on March 1, 1867, and he came to the United States in 1890. After two years near Greenwood, Mississippi, he came to Fort Pierce, Florida. A little later he moved down to West Palm Beach before moving to Miami in 1897. He began with a little store on Avenue D (Miami Avenue) near Fourteenth Street. His business interests grew rapidly. In September 1904 a three-story building was being raised on the Ullendorff block at Avenue D on Tenth Street, with stores on the first floor, offices on the second, and a meeting hall on the third. Two years later it was being replastered on the outside, and the Masons among others were

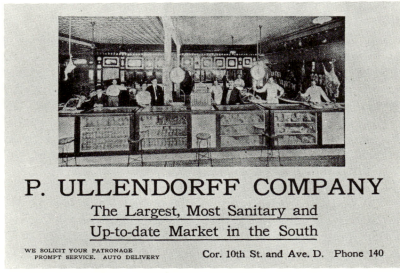

P. ULLENDORFF COMPANY
The Largest, Most Sanitary and
Up-to-date Market in the South

WE SOLICIT YOUR PATRONAGE
PROMPT SERVICE. AUTO DELIVERY

Cor. 10th St. and Ave. D. Phone 140

Advertisement for Ullendorff's meat market in 1915

meeting in the hall. Remodeling of the building in 1914 included the addition of a metal awning 170 feet long on the east side. In 1910 Ullendorff was making great improvements in his meat market at Avenue D and Tenth Street where he sold both salted and fresh meats. His advertisement for his business appeared regularly among the food ads as long as he lived. In 1910 he was also putting up a reinforced building with concrete floors for a steam laundry. The next year he sold a piece of property in Key West at the corner of Duval and Fleming streets for $15,000; a little over a year earlier he had purchased the same property for only $9,000. In 1912 he leased the Dixie Theater to the Greenwood Amusement Company of Atlanta and joined Dan Hardie and Walter Waldin in a project to build a six-story building on property at Eleventh Street and Avenue C, purchased from the Methodist Church. In 1913 he was credited with a 600 percent profit on a $30,000 deal.

In 1916 Ullendorff, through his friend Isidor Cohen, sold two hundred feet between Coconut Grove Road (South Bayshore Drive) and the bay for $25,000. The Ullendorffs had lived in a frame house on this property, but land in the area was being purchased by wealthy men for establishing estates. On one side was the James Deering Estate, Vizcaya.

Ullendorff had married Jennie Simpson of Astor, Florida, in Hamilton County on the St. Johns River. According to one report, she had nursed him through a severe case of yellow fever. In the summer of 1916 the Ullendorffs were entertaining Miamians at their summer home in Colorado Springs, which probably accounts for Isidor Cohen handling the real estate transactions that summer. Upon their return to the city, they resided at 536 Southwest 12th Avenue, where he died on September 10, 1923. Rabbi Julian Shapo of Temple Beth David officiated, and the pallbearers were Isidor Cohen, Harry Simons, J. H. Gilman, F. H. Wharton, A. H. Patten, C. B. Richards, and R. W. Gray.

In the second decade of the century a number of Key West families began to migrate to the Miami area. The extension of the Florida East Coast Railroad to Key West had not arrested the declining importance of that city. It had lost two of its principal industries, cigar manufacturing and the gathering, processing, and selling of natural sponges from nearby waters. The railroad had relieved all south Florida of dependence upon Key West for markets. One Key Wester, in fact, suggested that the railroad afforded them a chance to escape. The exodus from the Jewish community in Key West had devastating consequences for those who remained. In the early twenties the population dropped to about a dozen families. The small congregation could no longer afford the services of a rabbi, and for thirty years laymen conducted the services. Probably the most important of them was Joe Pearlman, who was president for twenty-five years from 1926 to 1952. His brother, Jules, was among the migrants to Miami who pioneered the Temple Israel congregation. Joe Pearlman later became honorary life president. During and since the Second World War the Jewish population in Key West has again grown to about what it was at the turn of the century. Synagogue services have been restored, and a new building combining synagogue, social hall, and rabbi's residence has been constructed. The current spiritual leader is Rabbi Nathan Zwitman, the brother of Temple Israel's rabbi from 1936 to 1949, Colman A. Zwitman. The rising fortunes of Miami attracted many of those leaving Key West. Among the names of families leaving Key West were Aronovitz, Blanck, Cassel, Engler, Fine, Kanner, Kirchik, Liebowitz, Louis, Margoles, Markovitch, Marks, Pearlman, Plikansky (Plant), Rippa, Rubin, Sable, Schoenfeld, Siegel, Steinberg, Weinstein, Weintraub, Wolfson, and Wolkowski.

Others came from New York to Miami at much the same time. Prominent among them was David Afremow who had established the New York Bargain Store in 1909. In 1913 he sold out to Dan Cromer. In time the store became Cromer and Cassel, and still later the present Richards Department Store. Morris L. Cowen in 1912 established the first of what was to become a chain of shoe stores.

Cromer-Cassel's New York Department Store on Miami Avenue and Northeast First Street, 1925

The growing population and the optimistic economic outlook helped the Miami Jews, after several premature starts, to effectively organize a congregation, call a rabbi, and acquire a synagogue. After the disastrous fire in December 1896 and the ensuing decline in the Jewish population, those who remained disbanded the organization that had been put together informally. In 1912 there were enough people with enough interest to try again. A dozen Jewish residents, Louis Fine, M. Zion, Lee Bergman, Samuel Cohen, J. Engler, Morris Plikansky, S. Abenson, A. Engler, Max Shaff, Max Dubler, and Isidor Cohen organized themselves into a congregation which they named B'nai Zion. In 1913 the establishment of the Young Men's Hebrew Association (YMHA) created a recreational, social, religious center for Jewish life. All groups met there until their numbers became too large or they had their own meeting places. A year earlier a section of the Miami City Cemetery on Northeast Second Avenue just south of the present Temple Israel site was set aside and dedicated as a Jewish burying ground.

Thereafter progress was slow but continuous. In 1915 women organized the Daughters of Israel to provide leadership in establishing various activities. This later became the Miami Chapter of the National Council of Jewish Women. On Friday evenings and Holy Days the congregation assembled in various public halls for religious services. In March 1916 when they met to celebrate the Feast of Purim, Isidor Cohen urged that it was time for them to have a synagogue. "There are," he said, "both synagogue and Temple Jews in Miami, but they will unite." The adjective "synagogue" referred to Orthodox, and "Temple" to Reform or other non-Orthodox groups. He was speaking hopefully for he knew there were already significant differences among Miami's Jewish population about the kind of Judaism that should be recognized.

In 1917 B'nai Zion was reorganized and received its charter as Temple Beth David. In the same year the congregation, with Philip Ullendorff as president, and the other officers, Dan Cromer, David Afremow, M. Zion, H. Schneidman, and Morris

Plikansky, purchased a site for a synagogue on the southeast corner of Avenue B and Fourth Street. Partly because the First World War intervened, building was delayed. In April 1920 they traded the lot for a building at Avenue H and Tenth Street which the First Christian Church was selling to move to a new location. The purchasers refurbished the building for their purposes, and it became Temple Beth David, Miami's first synagogue.

Miami's Jewish community was also being discovered as a source of money in national fund-raising efforts. In 1917 the first Relief for Jewish War Refugees was collected. The next year a long list of local donors contributed $224.50 to a relief fund for Jewish victims of the war. In 1921, the Immigrant Hebrew Shelter and Immigration Society of America sent Dr. H. Rosenzweig to seek participation in a $1,000,000 drive during the Jewish New Year celebration. Louis Fine, president of the

Temple Beth David, Miami, 1924

Temple Beth David congregation, and Isidor Cohen were to coordinate the effort.

Getting and keeping a rabbi for a small struggling congregation as usual proved difficult. Efforts to bring a spiritual leader to officiate at High Holy Days services were not usually successful because rabbis were in demand in more promising places. In 1918 Rabbi M. Samuelson officiated, but he did not remain very long. In 1921 Louis M. Levitsky of Montreal, Canada, a student at Schechter's Theological Seminary in New York, was guest rabbi at services attended by almost 500 people, the greater part of the Jewish community. Shortly thereafter, Dr. Salo Stein had a one-year tenure as Temple Beth David's spiritual leader, but in January 1923 he began working with a group to organize Temple Israel. Dr. Stein was also planning a huge sanitarium, hotel, and apartment complex on Miami Beach. Apparently he left the rabbinate for the real estate business during the land boom. In the fall of 1923, when Louis Fine died, Temple Beth David lost the layman who most nearly held the status of spiritual leader. In that year Rabbi Julian Shapo came to Miami for a two-year stay. He came from Knoxville, Tennessee, and had served previously at Newport News, Virginia, Tampa, Florida, and Key West. The coming of Rabbi Murray Alstet in 1925 to succeed Shapo marked the establishment of continuous spiritual leadership.

The final achievement of a fully operative organization did not, as Isidor Cohen had hopefully stated, result in harmony among Miami's Jews. It may well have served to sharpen the differences and set the stage for the three-way division that soon occurred. Temple Beth David began as a Conservative congregation, but strong Orthodox elements were in it. The first to pull out, though, were supporters of the Reform interpretation of Judaism who founded Temple Israel in 1922. In the continuing struggle between Conservative and Orthodox members within Temple Beth David, the Orthodox achieved ascendancy for a brief time but finally pulled out and later formed the first Orthodox congregation in Miami, and Temple Beth David remained Conservative. In 1925 and 1926 the three groups each held High Holy Day services. Rabbi Shapo had left Temple Beth David and was holding an Orthodox service in the Masonic Hall. Rabbi Murray Alstet was officiating at Temple Beth David. The Temple Israel congregation was meeting in its own Temple in 1925 but was again in temporary quarters in the Central Grammar School auditorium in the fall of 1926.

The Orthodox group was organized as Miami Orthodox Congregation in 1931, later as Miami Hebrew Congregation, and finally as Temple Beth El. In 1926 a different Orthodox group had organized a congregation on Miami Beach which took the name Beth Jacob and acquired a synagogue in 1929.

3/Orthodoxy and Reform: Common Ends, Differing Means

By the year 1922 the Jewish community in Miami had become large enough and sufficiently well established to effect fairly stable congregational organizations and permanent religious institutions. It was also the circumstance in which the differences inherent in Judaism in the United States in the twentieth century began to emerge. Jews are in substantial agreement about what they wish to accomplish, but they differ widely over ways to achieve the goal. They wish to preserve their identity, which includes along with their religion, and certainly not apart from it, a cultural, ethical, and historical heritage. They have preserved their identity for centuries while scattered over the world, often suffering persecution as well as discrimination. These pressures on them as an alien minority in a hostile environment have in fact had much to do with their standing closely together to preserve that heritage.

In the United States with its pluralistic society the quest for survival and acceptance has been won, thereby releasing much of the pressure that has held the Jewish people together. Now an even greater danger faces them. It is the possibility of assimilation and secularization in a world changing at an accelerated rate. How shall the challenge to the Hebrew heritage be met? Some Jews frankly accept assimilation as the answer. They do not so much reject Judaism as simply abandon it as being no longer useful to them. At the other extreme, the response is a commitment to strict orthodoxy in ideology, ritual, and practice, a reaffirmation of ancient and honored forms and spirit, a refusal to yield anything to the new forces hammering away at them. Yet another approach is the effort to come to terms with the contemporary world but hold on to historical Jewish ethical, moral, and religious values.

Miami's first Jewish congregation elected the Conservative route to the common objective, but there were also strong Orthodox influences within Temple Beth David. The Orthodox members felt they could make little or no concession to modern influences in personal and religious life, and they proposed to survive by clinging to traditional ways that had kept Judaism alive against great hazards for a long time. The new hazards might be quite different from ones in the past, but the Orthodox members had the advantage that the roles they would play were long established and well defined. Those Jews who elected to achieve the same ends by change and adjustment to save that which they considered to be the essence of Judaism were running the risk that they might lose what they were attempting to preserve, but they counted the achievement worth the risk.

The elements in Orthodoxy from which a growing number of Jews dissented had to do more with practices than with beliefs, more to do with means than with ends. The dissidents revered the Torah as deeply as any, but they in varying degrees emphasized the spirit rather than the forms of Judaic law.

Reform Judaism originated in Germany in the nineteenth century and came with German immigrants to the United States where it found more fertile ground in which to grow. Its founding father in this country was Rabbi Isaac Mayer Wise. He wished American Jewry to be led by rabbis born and educated in America. Most likely he was more interested in an American rabbinate than in the conflict being waged between Orthodox and Reform forces. Up to that time spiritual leaders had come from abroad and usually could not speak English. More important, he felt that they could not think or feel in the American spiritual and intellectual idiom. He saw the character of both the congregation and the rabbinate to be determined to a great degree by what was going on in American society. To these ends he founded Hebrew Union College, the first Jewish seminary in the United States, in Cincinnati in 1875 to train rabbis for Reform congregations and to offer advice and counsel to Reform Jews in the field.

Reform, if the word be rendered literally, is something of a misnomer when applied to Jewish Reform congregations. If reform means return to some original state of purity, Mosaism as it were, the word certainly does not describe Reform Judaism. A comparable confusion of terms is the Lutheran Protestant Reformation which became in reality more of a revolution. Martin Luther began with an effort to achieve reform, to shed accretions to original doctrine and practice, to return to the original character of the Christian religion. Others seized the movement to achieve revolutionary changes. Reform Judaism is neither a return to strict Mosaism nor a revolution from the Orthodox. It is an effort to escape from the view held by many non-Jewish historians and, by implication at least, some Jews, that nothing has changed since the beginning of the Christian Era.

In terms which are largely those of Dr. Joseph R. Narot, senior rabbi of Temple Israel since 1950, Reform Judaism holds that the Bible is not so much the final revealed work of God as it is the record of man's historic quest for the word of God. Rituals are not so much sacraments which forever damn by the violation of them and bless by the fulfillment of them as they are aesthetic symbols of ideals men espouse. Man shares in the messianic ideal that all men of every faith, race, and nation must labor together for the better life of justice and peace. Reform Judaism is not interested in the abolition of ceremony, but it does insist that ceremonies be effective as means of religious culture and that they be observed not as ends in themselves or with a view to obtaining rewards but as an expression of religious feeling. Some Reform Jews did feel that all Orthodox symbols should be abandoned, but have tended more recently to find ritual an important expression of religious feeling.

Far from seeing history end with the revelations in the Bible, Reform scholars proclaim history as the self-unfolding, self-revelation of God. They see revelation as a continuous process and the history of Judaism as displaying God in the continuous act of self-revelation. To them this places Judaism under the law of growth and implies change to meet changing circumstances.

In summary, a quotation from Dr. Solomon B. Freehof, President of the Central Conference of American Rabbis, printed in the Temple Israel *Bulletin* on January 5, 1945, serves admirably. He explained: "Reform Judaism proclaims the right of each generation to change customs and rituals and even to create doctrines provided essential principles of Judaism are preserved and strengthened by such changes. The same liberal principles which gave the Reform pioneers the right to change the venerable customs and prayer texts of Orthodoxy give us the right to change and modify doctrines of the pioneers.

"Any attempt to fix Reform Judaism at the pattern of one hundred years ago or fifty years ago petrifies it into Reformed Judaism, a form of Judaism which had at one time been Reformed and then remained forever fixed. . . . "

This new concept of Judaism has necessarily involved differences of opinion regarding the function of the synagogue and the role of the rabbi. The historic functions of prayer, study, and assembly remain in the synagogue. The ancient synagogue was also a great mutual aid society. It provided dowries for poor Jewish brides, decent burial for the indigent, hospitality for transients, ransom for captives, healing for the sick, and comfort for mourners. It was the one haven to which the Jew could bring all the problems arising from his exclusion from the larger community in which he lived. Today many of these services have been institutionalized outside the synagogue. Hospitals, family agencies, burial societies, and federations provide services, but the sense of communal responsibility for the welfare of every individual remains and spills over into the non-Jewish community as well.

Writing in *The Jewish Floridian* of March 11, 1960, Leo Mindlin commented that the traditional rabbis of eastern Europe dealt principally with questions pertaining directly to Jewish literature, law, and lore. Their modern counterparts, on the other hand, frequently base sermons and counsel, as well as leadership, on a working knowledge of current events. Their viewpoints are fashioned by the predominant qualities of the congregation whose pulpits they occupy. Contrast with this an article in the same journal on July 12, 1962, which argues that synagogue leaders should relieve the rabbi of such functions as business administration, fund raising, and glorified public relations so that he can be restored to a position of spiritual authority and persuasiveness.

The word leader is a correct designation of the status of the rabbi. A congregation is usually organized by a group of laymen, although a rabbi may at times participate. Government of the congregation remains with the temple board of trustees and the congregation. The board, with the approval of the congregation, employs the rabbi, fixes his salary, and then determines his tenure, thereby deciding the direction in which the group will go. Such organizations as Hebrew Union College, the Union of America Hebrew Congregations, and Hillel Foundation and prominent rabbis or other individuals may assist in recruiting candidates, but the final authority belongs to the congregation.

This is not to suggest that once the rabbi is chosen he is not an all important part of the organization. The role he plays depends partly on the attitude of the temple board but more upon his own personality and talents as a leader. In any case, the rabbi brings to the position all the tradition of the rabbi as scholar, teacher, preacher, and spiritual leader, and the pulpit is recognized as peculiarly his own. By its very nature Reform Judaism tends to make the rabbi a full partner in the enterprise. The office at Temple Israel has gone through a steady evolution in that direction.

The word spiritual in the description of the rabbi's leadership must be very broadly construed to cover the wide range of interests and activities of many Reform rabbis. Some spokesmen for Judaism insist that the secular aspects of congregational affairs should be handled completely by laymen, leaving the rabbi the purely spiritual or religious functions of his office. This idea is also peculiarly characteristic of many of the evangelical sects in American Protestantism. The members feel that a minister who becomes involved in political or social issues, even those of vital importance to their own welfare, somehow loses his effectiveness for their more important spiritual leadership. Certainly at times this has been an important issue at Temple Israel.

Opinion and practice differ widely as to the extent to which a rabbi owes his time and energy to the congregation. How much should he reasonably be expected to do in the way of community service, non-Jewish as well as with his coreligionists? Reform rabbis, at least those at Temple Israel, have been increasingly involved in all aspects of Temple affairs and in community affairs. In this last respect, they may be said thereby to have won distinction for themselves and for Temple Israel.

In another area of great concern, Jewish Orthodoxy tends to look upon Palestine not merely as the cradle but also as the ultimate home of Judaism. Reform Judaism conceives of the destiny of the people of Israel as not necessarily bound up in a return to the State of Israel, and as certainly not involving national political restoration under a messianic king with the Temple rebuilt and the sacrificial service reinstituted. This concept, however, does not prevent Reform Jews from generously contributing money and skills to the survival and development of Israel as an independent and self-sufficient national entity.

It would be a serious error to leave the impression that the explanation of differences among Jews lies exclusively in the realm of religious beliefs. Other considerations—residential, occupational, social, and personal—may lead to secessions and divisions. The direction a new congregation takes, Orthodox, Conservative, Reform, Liberal, or Reconstructionist, is, however, largely a religious decision.

The congregational form of church government so congenial to the American mind that it has modified the authority of centralized and hierarchical bodies made it easy for any group to set up an organization tailored to its own wishes and interests. The influence of congregational church government in all religious groups in American life has been far more pervasive and continuous than the equally important New England town meeting of colonial days as an ingredient in American democracy. Literally each temple might have its own reason for being. There is no "national rabbi," no hierarchy that exercises any authority. This is not to suggest that complete autonomy exists among Reform temples. A degree of unity among Reform Jewish congregations is achieved through the influence of the Hebrew Union College described earlier. The Jewish Institute of Religion in New York, now affiliated with Hebrew Union College, contributes to the same ends. The federation of Reform temples in the Union of American Hebrew Congregations also helps to establish common grounds for teaching and practice. The same may be said for the Central Conference of American Rabbis.

It should be emphasized that the same Jews who distribute themselves among several temples to give expression to their differences also come together to achieve common purposes. These include education, charity, hospital and cultural and social service, and fund raising for common causes.

In this context, conceding that there may also have been purely personal and local reasons for the secession, it was completely consistent with Jewish practice to establish a new and different congregation in Miami in 1922. Had the prospect of community growth and affluence not been so rosy at the time, or if those involved could have seen what the near future would bring, they might have hesitated to make the move at that time. That the move would occur was inherent in the state of Judaism at the time and made easy by American practice.

4/ Miami's First Jewish Reform Congregation

The history of the early informal steps leading to the formation of the new congregation must be pieced together out of scanty records and recollections of events a half century old. General agreement is that Harry V. Simons, who became the first president, was the prime mover. The date of formal organization is variously reported largely because of differences as to which of a long series of meetings should be designated "first." May 1922 was accepted as the birth date in 1947 when the silver anniversary was being celebrated, and large numbers of founders, including Harry Simons, were still around. Joseph Faus, writing historically and reminiscently years later, was more specific when he put the date at May 18, 1922, but without explanation. There must have been several earlier meetings, any one of which might have been called the first important one, for it is clear that almost two years of preliminary work preceded the approval of the charter on May 31, 1923. Sie Mendelson, who came to Miami from New Orleans in the summer of 1921, recalls that soon after his arrival he was invited to join the new group. This suggests that the meeting called at the home of Morris Cowen to inaugurate the movement for a new congregation must have occurred not later than the fall of 1921. In attendance besides Cowen at this first meeting were Morris Gusky, Dr. M. D. Katz, J. Gerald Lewis, Sie Mendelson, Morris Plant, Nat Roth, Harry V. Simons, Philip Ullendorff, Louis Wolfson, and Louis Zeientz, of whom three (Lewis, Mendelson, and Roth) lived to participate in the golden anniversary celebration. Temporary officers elected at this first meeting were Simons as president, Katz as vice-president, Gusky as secretary, and Plant as treasurer.

Another authoritative record of a "first" meeting with a different date, which really implies a different kind of first, is in a letter of Harry Simons to the Union of American Hebrew Congregations (UAHC) in Cincinnati, dated July 24, 1923. It reads in part: "For the past several years there has been a strong felt want for a reform movement in Miami but it was not until September 1922 that the feeling ripened and took form in the organization of Temple Israel." This September date is further documented by an incomplete series of accounts, actually minutes, of congregational meetings, sometimes two in a month. The report dated March 1923 is designated the eighth meeting. At the ninth meeting, also in March at the home of Dr. Salo Stein, it was reported that everything was in readiness for the reorganization of the Sunday school. At the fourteenth meeting in August held in the home of Harry Simons, the resignation of Dr. Stein as rabbi was accepted. Unfortunately, the minutes for the next several years are missing.

There is also an intriguing newspaper account of a meeting on January 7, 1923. On the next day *The Miami Herald* reported that a new congregation had been organized on the previous evening. Harry Simons was reported as the temporary president, Abe Aronovitz as treasurer (the only time that Aronovitz's name appears as an officer), and Nat Roth as secretary. It was also reported that Dr. Salo Stein, who had served Temple Beth David as spiritual leader in 1922, had been elected "acting rabbi." It could be assumed that this meeting was the one at which the decision to apply for a charter was made. Thirty-nine names appear on the charter but with some changes among the officeholders. Simons is named president; Gusky, secretary; Plant, treasurer; and Mrs. M. L. Cowen, financial secretary. For the names of other charter members, see appendix D.

The honor of naming the new congregation went to Philip Ullendorff, who was counted on heavily for financial support. He chose Israel because it was his father's name, and the name of the new congregation became Temple Israel Reform Jewish Congregation of Miami. One of the signers of the charter was Dr. Salo Stein. He served Temple Israel as spiritual leader for only a short time. On August 8, 1923, the Temple Board of Trustees accepted his resignation from the pulpit, but made him and his wife honorary life members. Some members and prospective members rejected his leadership because of his earlier association with Temple Beth David. Only Mendelson of the original eleven had not been a member of the older congregation. Stein remained active, as indicated by the minutes of a meeting of the congregation in his home on January 31, 1924. Like so many others from all walks of life he became a real estate operator during the boom that followed.

In the fall of 1923 Rabbi Louis I. Egelson, assistant director of the UAHC, came from Cincinnati to officiate at High Holy Days services. He had been consulted by the organizers in the previous year. During his stay he helped the Sisterhood to organize and supplied a model constitution. He conferred with the Temple board on several problems of the new congregation, not the least of which was obtaining the services of a rabbi. On September 13 the board decided they might be able to pay from $2,000 to $2,500 a year and voted to start the search. In a letter to the president of Hebrew Union College (HUC), they reported they had thirty-eight members and thought the number might quickly grow to seventy-five if they had a spiritual leader. An estimated 250 Jewish families were in the area, the greater part of them unaffiliated, and the winter season would bring up to 1,000 seasonal residents and visitors. In a letter to the UAHC, the secretary of the congregation was apparently rejecting a suggestion that the Miami group affiliate with West Palm Beach. He pointed out that West Palm Beach was seventy-five miles away and already well organized. At the end of November the UAHC office was reminding the fledgling congregation that the financial report was due!

Largely by chance the small congregation secured the services of a rabbi. On December 4, 1923, the board received word that Rabbi Joseph Jasin was available. He was a graduate of HUC and had served at Fort Worth, Texas, and Pine Bluff, Arkansas. He was available only because he was returning to the ministry after having given it up for a time. Two days later the Miami congregation invited him. He did not prove to be the hoped for "permanent rabbi." The congregation and Rabbi Jasin parted company shortly after Sukkot in 1925. The Temple Israel Board of Trustees refused responsibility for a medical bill he built up at Jackson Memorial Hospital after his resignation or dismissal but later voted him $825 to help pay his transportation to California. Dr. Katz, assisted by other laymen, took responsibility for services, and the search for a rabbi started over again.

Rabbi Jasin, in his short time at Temple Israel, organized the Friendship League to merge all the social and philanthropic activities of the young men and women in the Jewish community. Leaders in the enterprise were Adel Letaw, who later became Mrs. Sidney Beskind; George Wolpert, who was president, and Mrs. C. W. Bowman, who acted as hostess on social occasions. Although its membership was not restricted to the Temple Israel congregation, the organization met in the Fourteenth Street synagogue until it was dismantled and at times participated in Temple services. After Temple Israel moved, the League was never again associated with it. For a time the Friendship League met in the hall of the Biscayne Lodge Masonic Temple at Northwest First Street and Thirteenth Avenue. In January 1927, *The Miami News* reported a meeting and dance at which officers were installed. Magazines were being distributed to hospital wards and athletic events were sponsored. These activities in time became institutionalized, and such volunteer organizations lost their reason for being.

Besides their search for a rabbi, Temple Israel was also looking for cemetery lots. Burials had previously been in a section set aside in the Miami City Cemetery on Northeast Second Avenue just south of the present Temple site. The cemetery committee took immediate steps to secure a block of lots in Woodlawn Cemetery. On September 25, 1923, the board approved borrowing $1,000 from the building fund to use as the first payment on lots to cost a total of $5,250.

During the preliminary stages of organization the founders of the new congregation met at first in the homes of members. Then they began to hold meetings in the Young Men's Hebrew Association (YMHA) rooms on the second floor of the Seybold Building on Flagler Street, which at the time was only two stories high. Of the YMHA Jules Pearlman recalled that he had been both president and janitor at that time. The board's minutes include a formal action to use the rooms for High Holy Days services in 1923, suggesting that meetings were still being held in homes except on special occasions. They also met for a time in the Woman's Club Building on lower Flagler Street where the Walgreen Drugstore on Flagler Street now stands.

All the while the congregation was looking for property of their own. Philip Ullendorff offered two lots on Southwest Twelfth Avenue and Fourth Street for a synagogue site. The location did not please the board. Twelfth Avenue was at the extreme western limit of the city and much of the intervening area was not yet developed. Most of the members lived in the Miramar section in which the Temple now stands. Ullendorff agreed that the lots might be sold and proceeds applied to the purchase of a more suitable site. The lot chosen was 275 Northeast Fourteenth Street out in what is now Biscayne Boulevard. The building that was erected was only a temporary structure, and the cost of the lot and all the equipment did not exceed $19,000. The frame building was small, 30 feet by 100 feet, and designed to seat about 300 persons. An office for the rabbi was located on a balcony. The structure was without any conventional windows. Described as "boxy" and looking like a barn or tobacco loft, it was actually a realistic adjustment to climate and circumstances. The walls, except those of the front, were

Original Temple Israel, 1924-26, from a drawing made in 1971 by Sie Mendelson

boarded up only about halfway to the roof, and the remainder was screened to provide ventilation and keep out mosquitoes. Curtains could be rolled down on the inside to keep out sunlight, and great hinged shutters on the outside could be lowered to shut out the rain or to close the building. Although the congregation did not know that this building was to serve only a short time, they did have their own place of worship for awhile, and such notables as William Jennings Bryan and his daughter Ruth were frequent visitors. Morris Plant, J. S. Aber, J. M. Gusky, H. I. Homa, Sie Mendelson, and Harry V. Simons made up the building committee. The building of the Ark was in a sense a community enterprise. Architect H. George Fink of Coral Gables fame designed it; The Paula Art Shops constructed it; and the John B. Orr Company did the painting.

The new sanctuary was shown to the public in an open house on Thursday, September 27, 1924, and used for the first time on the following evening as High Holy Days services began. The congregation dedicated the small synagogue at ceremonies on the last days in February 1925. At the first session the featured speakers were William Jennings Bryan, Miss Sophia Irene Loeb, and Judge Adolph Kraus, president of the Jewish World Fraternity, B'nai B'rith. At the Friday evening service Dr. Gustave N. Hausman preached on "The Synagogue in Jewish Life." On Sunday morning Sie Mendelson, vice-president, delivered an address of welcome, M. D. Katz, past president, described the beginnings of the congregation, and Morris Plant, the third president, discussed the present and the future as he saw it. Mrs. Plant, president of the Temple Sisterhood, discussed the role of that organization. Silas Inchenhauser of Evansville, Indiana, then talked about "Miami's Opportunity."

As it turned out the new building was directly in the roadway of developing Miami. The Phipps estate, which was developing Miami Shores, was buying the right-of-way for a wide street to downtown Miami that became known as Biscayne Boulevard.

Sie Mendelson recalls that a broker representing the purchasers approached him with an offer of $100,000 for the site. He was only the vice-president, and the president was out of town. He doubted the seriousness of the offer but replied that the congregation probably would not sell for even twice that amount. The offer soon became $200,000. When the congregation met to consider the proposal to sell, they decided that a sum should be added to cover closing costs and fees, and the selling price became $215,000. The sale was announced on August 14, 1925, but the congregation continued to use the building until the end of May 1926 when the purchasers were ready to tear it down. The board, meeting on June 3, suspended services for June and July. In August a new rabbi was to arrive, and services would be resumed in temporary quarters. After using the building for less than two years the congregation decided to abandon it rather than to move it to the new site. In fact, they had already outgrown the concept of temporary quarters of their own and meant to build accordingly. They sold the $1,400 worth of seats for $450, and they secured permission to store the Torah in the Ark at Temple Beth David. The ladies of the Sisterhood packed the moveable property, and Temple

Israel went shopping for a new temporary meeting place. They contracted for the use of the Central Grammar School auditorium, on the site of the present Federal Building, from August 1926 to August 1927, after which they accepted the offer of the Seventh Day Adventists to use their church until the new Temple was ready.

The proceeds of the sale were invested in government securities and thus escaped the chance that a part if not all might have been lost when the banks failed. Only one Miami bank survived without reorganization, and others never reopened. The building committee proceeded immediately to look for a new site and recommended two lots at 137 Northeast Nineteenth Street. Louis Wolfson was the lone objector, arguing that the boom had raised prices too high and that they would soon come down. He also disliked the location; it was an inside lot and too near the railroad. He felt that the site should be located on a main thoroughfare to provide easy access. He did later receive the support of the president of the Temple Brotherhood on the same grounds. The congregation approved the acquisition of the two lots at a cost of $70,000.

The desirability of the location has been debated many times since, particularly when the area began to deteriorate residentially and the board had to fight rezoning for business. The Temple received an ally when the School Board acquired the property westward on both sides of the street and built Miramar Elementary School on the north side. The City of Miami owned the property across the street to the south between the school property and Southeast Second Avenue. When the population began to move into suburban areas, some members who were moving thought that the Temple should follow them and locate in one of the suburbs, letting the remainder of the congregation join one of the new congregations sure to arise throughout Greater Miami. Others felt that Temple Israel should establish branch or satellite congregations where a sufficient number of Reform-minded Jews lived. The decision of the board, ratified by the congregation, to remain in the central city and draw membership from the whole area was one of the most critical ever made, and the reason for the change of name in 1957 to Temple Israel of Greater Miami. By that date the greater part of the membership lived outside the city limits of Miami, the greatest portion in Miami Beach.

In 1926, with more money in the building fund and more credit than they would have again for a long time, and undaunted by the onset of the depression after the collapse of the land boom in 1926, the members voted to go ahead with building plans at the Nineteenth Street site. This move did infuse new spirit into the members, but had they foreseen how long and difficult the struggle for solvency would be they might well have hesitated. As it was, they were able to complete the structure and make it ready for use by borrowing only $35,000. On October 26, 1926, the congregation authorized the building committee to proceed. Work began with the ground-breaking ceremonies on May 1. Morris Plant, president of the congrega-

Morris Plant breaking ground, May 1, 1927

tion, turned the first spadeful of dirt, and other officers and previous officers each took a turn. The laying of the cornerstone was delayed until near the High Holy Days. When the appointed day for the ceremony, October 16, arrived, the Masonic Order would not participate because the walls were almost completed. On the same day at 3:00 P.M. a special first meeting of the congregation on the ground floor or basement of the new structure was held, but no effort was made to hold High Holy Day services there that year. Meanwhile, on May 11, 1926, all 215 members of the congregation were elected to the newly named and chartered Temple Israel of Miami.

In a three-day series of ceremonies, February 17-19, 1928, the proud congregants dedicated their new sanctuary. On the first day at the Temple, city officials were the special guests. On the second, guests from farther afield were the honorees at the

Temple Israel, main sanctuary, dedicated in 1928 and still the principal house of worship for the congregation in 1972

Temple ceremonies. The third day featured a gala dinner meeting of the congregation at the Miami Biltmore Country Club in Coral Gables.

While the plans for the new building were under way, the search for a rabbi continued. In the expansive middle twenties the board believed that a salary of $8,000 to $8,500 should be offered to a suitable candidate. President of the Board of Trustees Louis A. Zeientz at a meeting in April 1926 gave the task of finding a spiritual leader to three men, Day J. Apte, Herbert U. Feibelman, and Sie Mendelson. The trio, immediately dubbed the "Three Wise Men from the South," journeyed to Cincinnati, to the national headquarters of Reform Judaism at HUC and UAHC for advice and counsel. Dr. Julian Morgenstern, president of HUC, suggested that Dr. Jacob H. Kaplan, rabbi at one of the city's Reform temples, might be interested. The three seekers went to hear Rabbi Kaplan preach and liked what they heard. Kaplan was interested. The committee recommended that he be employed at $8,000 a year, and the congregation approved on May 11, 1926.

A separate chapter, chapter six, is devoted to the role of Rabbi Kaplan as religious leader. It is sufficient at this point to note that he was fifty-two years old and brought a varied experience to the still very young and inexperienced congregation. He had been attracted by the building program and the promise for the future that spokesmen for the Temple conveyed.

Dr. and Mrs. Kaplan arrived in Miami on August 20, 1926, passengers on the steamer *Martha Weems*. On Friday, September 3, he preached his first sermon in the Central School Auditorium. Two weeks later, on the 17th, on the eve of the Day of Atonement, a tropical storm was obviously brewing, but the weather bureau advised that the congregation might proceed with the service. After the service, the worshippers made their way home in ominously increasing winds. Before morning the disastrous hurricane had come and gone, leaving ruin in its wake and undreamed consequences to follow. The sermon prepared for the 18th was not delivered. Any observance of the holy day was private.

Three barges washed up on Biscayne Boulevard by the 1926 hurricane

In the years following 1926 the Florida depression continued to worsen. Temple Israel, like most other institutions and many individuals, entered this difficult period seriously overcommitted. Sources of support dried up; retrenchment all along the line was the order of the day. Secretarial service for Kaplan was reduced to three afternoons a week. Search for a less expensive office rent was instituted. The paid choir was reduced to the organist and a soprano, but the congregation had started with a volunteer choir, so this was nothing new to most of the members. The six teachers in the religious school were asked to serve without pay, a condition that lasted well into 1929.

The printed program of the graduation of the first confirmation class on June 5, 1927, reveals something of congregational activity. The seventeen members of the class were confirmed by Rabbi Kaplan at the Seventh Day Adventist Church, and a reception followed at the Robert Clay Hotel. One of the group, Janice Brill, recalled in 1972 that Bea Weinstein taught them in

1925 and 1926 at the Temple. The next year Frank Pearlman instructed on Sundays at the Adventist Church, and Rabbi Kaplan met them one afternoon a week in a frame building for Boy Scouts in a park at Nineteenth Street and Northeast Second Avenue. Leonard Epstein continued their education for a postconfirmation year of study. Members of that first class were Alice Apte, Janice Brill, Arthur Cohen, Gertrude Dietz, Louise Dietz, Claire Freedman, Jerome Goldsmith, Gertrude Isenberg, Sara Ada Isenberg, Helen Kantor, Ellis B. Klein, Bertha Leibovit, Mindell Rothenberg, Ben Strauss, Sydel Hortense Swieg, Daniel Taradash, and Bernard Weintraub. The choir, directed by the organist, Mrs. Iva Sproul Baker, was made up of Mrs. H. U. Feibelman, designated "special" which meant soloist, Mrs. Jacob H. Kaplan, Mrs. Sie Mendelson, Mrs. M. L. Cowen, Mrs. Max Dobrin, Mrs. J. S. Wool, and Mrs. Beulah Greenhut.

Neither the rabbi's salary nor payment on the building debt was being made. Just how much of Dr. Kaplan's salary was

Nine of the seventeen members of Temple Israel's first confirmation class in 1927. Although the class was confirmed in June in the Seventh Day Adventist Church, this photograph was made in September in the new Temple. Left to right: Bernard Weintraub, Sara Isenberg, Gertrude Dietz, Arthur Cohen, Rabbi Kaplan, Bertha Leibovit, Helen Kantor, Louise Dietz, Gertrude Isenberg, and Ellis Klein.

actually being paid is difficult to determine. He volunteered to have it reduced from $8,000 to $6,000 a year, but it is doubtful that that much was being paid. On May 1, 1931, the congregation voted him life tenure at a salary of at least $5,000 a year to be paid whenever the congregation was able financially to do so. On September 1, 1935, the life tenure contract was dissolved by mutual consent, and his back pay at the promised $5,000 a year was calculated and promised to him and paid soon thereafter, although not all at one time.

The change of tenure was preliminary to plans to employ an assistant rabbi who could perhaps succeed Dr. Kaplan at a later date. On April 8, 1936, the board moved to employ an assistant rabbi and social director. The secretary wrote HUC President Julian Morgenstern, Rabbi Stephen S. Wise, and the director of the Hillel Foundation for nominations. They accepted the recommendation of Rabbi Wise and elected one of his protégés, Colman A. Zwitman, who at the time was serving a congregation in Bluefield, West Virginia. His coming to Temple Israel in 1936 paved the way for Rabbi Kaplan's retirement in 1941, and Zwitman became the senior rabbi. Dr. Kaplan accepted emeritus status at $3,600 a year with promise of support for his wife if she survived him. But Rabbi Kaplan's services to the congregation were far from done. The grateful congregation paid him full salary when he came out of retirement several times to fill in until a rabbi could be secured and voted him bonuses from time to time. Clearly his income never again rose to what his contract called for in the first years. Nor had the members of the congregation yet recovered the expectations of the middle twenties.

The United States entered World War II on December 8, 1941. On January 5, 1943, HUC, which recruited Jewish chaplains for the armed services, requested that retired rabbis be asked to fill pulpits left temporarily vacant by rabbis in the service of the government. At the time Rabbi Zwitman had no reason to expect that he would be asked to volunteer for the armed services, but the Temple board asked Dr. Kaplan to stand by and not accept a bid to go elsewhere. Zwitman had been unofficial chaplain to thirty-two Jewish men at Officers' Candidate School on Miami Beach and to another three men at Opa-locka.

Eventually Rabbi Zwitman did enter the army as a chaplain in 1943 and was absent for three years. On March 9 he announced his intention to become a chaplain, but actually received the commission several months later. To employ a rabbi for the duration of the conflict was, of course, next to impossible. Rabbi Kaplan took over, but he was not expected to assume the full responsibility for a long period. On February 1, 1944, the board's first choice finally declined. Later in the same month Rabbi Jacob Tarshish accepted a call to Miami. At the same time Temple Israel agreed to pay the difference between Rabbi Zwitman's pay as a chaplain and his salary as rabbi. Rabbi Tarshish resigned effective September 1, 1944, for reasons of health, but agreed to remain through the High Holy Days, for which Dr. Kaplan also returned to duty. Kaplan served until November 21, when Rabbi Saul Applebaum accepted the position of associate rabbi for the duration of Zwitman's absence but not less than one year. Applebaum was formerly assistant rabbi to Dr. Jonah B. Wise of the Central Synagogue in New York City and had become regional rabbi of the UAHC, an ideal position from which to take a temporary assignment. On April 18, 1946, Rabbi Zwitman wrote that he was released from the army and awaiting the word of Temple Israel to return on June 15. Rabbi Applebaum, as agreed in his contract, resigned as of the same date.

Colman Zwitman was never to recover from the consequences of his war service. He had contracted a liver ailment while stationed in the Philippines, and it eventually became malignant. He reported his health problem on January 1, 1947, but declined a leave of absence. Although he managed to perform most of his duties, he grew progressively weaker until his death on December 3, 1949.

As early as May 6, 1947, the board considered appointing an assistant rabbi. Six hundred members were too much for one rabbi. Two months later they arranged with Rabbi Emeritus

Kaplan to officiate during Zwitman's vacation. When Rabbi Zwitman died, Dr. Kaplan, then seventy-five years old, performed his last really arduous service for Temple Israel. Although visiting rabbis and other notables did some preaching during the early part of the year 1950, Dr. Kaplan did the greater part of the preaching until Rabbi Joseph R. Narot arrived in August. Happily, Dr. Kaplan lived another fifteen years to see the Temple finally emerge from depression and war and begin to realize some of what he had hoped when he came in 1926. That it was under new leadership did not make him unhappy.

One other legacy of the depression remained to be cleared away before Temple Israel could move ahead. As early as July 1932 the Temple board instructed the finance committee to negotiate with the trustees of the bondholders to reduce the principal and interest on the debt. Even though this was common practice by distressed individuals and institutions, public and private, the committee had little success. Finally on January 10, 1934, the board appointed an executive committee to settle the bonded indebtedness and balance the budget and get the Temple going again on its religious mission. Max Orovitz was chairman, and members were Gerald Lewis, Leonard Epstein, and H. U. Feibelman. The bondholders held out for $29,000 in settlement of the mortgage. This amount proved to be beyond the credit resources of the Temple, but the committee came up with a solution. In 1935 a new mortgage was arranged with Jefferson Standard Life Insurance Company for $18,000, but in addition to a mortgage on the Temple property, forty members of the congregation purchased $9,100 of "baby bonds." Ten years later the final payment of the mortgage was made, and all the baby bonds had been turned in as donations.

The personal lives and spiritual leadership of Dr. Kaplan and Rabbi Zwitman receive separate treatment in chapters six and seven.

5/A Quarter Century
of Growth, 1947-1972

In 1947, at the end of its first twenty-five years, Temple Israel had at last recovered from two decades of depression and a World War that had dominated its existence. Like the State of Florida and Greater Miami, it stood on the brink of an era of expansion that made the booming twenties pale into insignificance by contrast. By 1972 Dade County had as many people as were in all Florida in 1925. There was less of the bizarre and the purely speculative in the growth of the fifties and sixties. This age of affluence brought not only new people but more adequate financial resources to meet some of the opportunities and challenges of a complex metropolitan area. It was as if the end of the conflict had released all the creative energies that had been marshaled to win the war, producing a golden age of material achievement.

Temple Israel did not escape the problems that sprang up like mushrooms in the postwar generation. The Temple was not to be an oasis of calm and contemplation; rather, it was more often in the very thick of the conflicts and controversies that raged throughout the land over civil rights, minority rights, urban blight and efforts at renewal, the desegregation crisis, the

Negro revolution, the growing protest against an unpopular war in East Asia, the threat to international peace in the Middle East, the worldwide youth rebellion, the alarming growth of drug use and addiction, the seeming decline in the influence of religion and its institutions, the widespread disenchantment with education as a reliable panacea for all ills, the threat to the ecological environment, and a tendency to violence that was highlighted by the assassination of a president, a U.S. senator campaigning for the presidency, and Martin Luther King, the symbol of the Negro's demand for identity and recognition.

The tempo of Temple life had been increasing during the war, but most action was delayed until after the conflict ended. Members found an outlet for their interests and energies in wartime service of various kinds. The Temple welcomed servicemen stationed in the area and contributed directly and indirectly to the refugee victims of the war. Wartime scarcity of labor and materials made anything but emergency repairs to existing buildings all but impossible.

In 1944 Herman Wall, chairman of the cemetery committee since 1938, reported that the committee had completed the purchase and improvement of Temple Israel Cemetery in Graceland Memorial Park and was making arrangements for perpetual-care contracts. The dedication was on May 29.

In 1945 the debt contracted in 1928 to complete and equip the interior of the one building the congregation owned and used was paid off. The mortgage-burning ceremony on December 26 marked the end of a long financial struggle. The first order of business was to improve the sanctuary by adding air conditioning, which was ready for use in July 1946.

The most insistent demand for new building was for the use of the religious school. Classes were being conducted in Kaplan Hall, the basement floor of the sanctuary. It was too small and ill adapted for the purpose. At the annual meeting in 1946 the board took full responsibility for financing the school and relieved the Sisterhood of the large share it had been providing. By 1950 an enrollment of 280 pupils made expanded quarters imperative. The Temple *Bulletin* on January 13 of that year announced: "A new building will be erected for the Temple Sunday School and will bear the name of 'The Colman A. Zwitman Religious School.' " The Sisterhood talked over the plans and committed all funds raised in the year for it; but, the school did not immediately materialize. In 1951 the board decided that the school should be located at the Temple site rather than on Miami Beach where a growing number of the members resided. Someone had obviously proposed that the school be located there. A further commitment to an expanded program of religious education was the employment of Jacob Bornstein in 1952 as cantor and director of the religious school. In December 1953 the congregation at the mid-year meeting authorized a building program to cost up to $350,000. In 1955 the new religious school was dedicated.

The proposal to add a cantor met some opposition, but support was also growing. As early as November 1939, Jack Bern-

Ground breaking for The Colman A. Zwitman Religious School, 1954

stein, in a meeting of the congregation, made a plea for more ritual in the service. Perhaps Rabbi Zwitman's singing had also softened the opposition to a cantor by demonstrating the dimension singing might add to the worship service. In other areas too there was growing recognition that ritual and ceremony could be a means to achieve satisfying religious experience. Bar mitzvah, never forbidden in Reform Judaism, was looked upon with more favor and became more and more common. Perhaps Reform Judaism was feeling more secure and less obligated to prove itself by renouncing all the symbols of Orthodoxy. The establishment of the State of Israel stimulated interest in the Hebrew language as Jews increasingly saw ritual and symbol as ways to maintain a link with their historic past.

Population growth raised other questions at Temple Israel. The increasing number of Jews on Miami Beach, who already constituted about half of Temple Israel's membership, made a move to establish a new congregation there very likely.

Some members at Temple Israel felt that a new congregation on Miami Beach should be a branch of the first Reform organization. This proposal was voted down twice in 1946, once by the Miami Beach members of the congregation. Also voted down was a proposal to hold High Holy Days services in a church or a theater on the Beach. In 1948 Temple Israel welcomed a new Reform Temple across Biscayne Bay, Temple Beth Sholom. The number of synagogues throughout the Greater Miami area continued to grow as Jews moved into the rapidly growing suburban areas. The leadership at Temple Israel, supported by the congregants, stuck to the idea that they should remain in the central city and draw members from the entire region. To that end they debated a name change in May and adopted the present name Temple Israel of Greater Miami in November 1957.

In May 1949 the membership had reached 668 families. The Temple seated a maximum of 850 persons and Kaplan Hall seated another 400. Until some new arrangement could be made for High Holy Days services, the congregation was already as large as could be accommodated. And always a large number of unaffiliated Jews wished to participate. The decision that year to hold dual services relieved the pressure on space enough for the membership committee again to become active. But dual and even triple services, using a visiting rabbi and a second cantor, at the Northeast Nineteenth Street facility soon became both insufficient and unsatisfactory. Seventeen separate services in 1962 resulted in the decision to try Miami Beach Convention Hall the next year. After the experiment in 1963 the membership voted about eighty percent approval of the move. Close to 4,500 persons now worship together at one time on High Holy Days. This is not to suggest that the congregation would not prefer their own sanctuary, but if families cannot worship together and guests cannot be accommodated in their sanctuary, then they yield to circumstances. The attachment of the members to their own sanctuary was shown when the confirmation classes became so large that the family attendance had to be restricted, and parents voted in December 1963 to keep the

High Holy Day service in Miami Beach Convention Hall, 1968

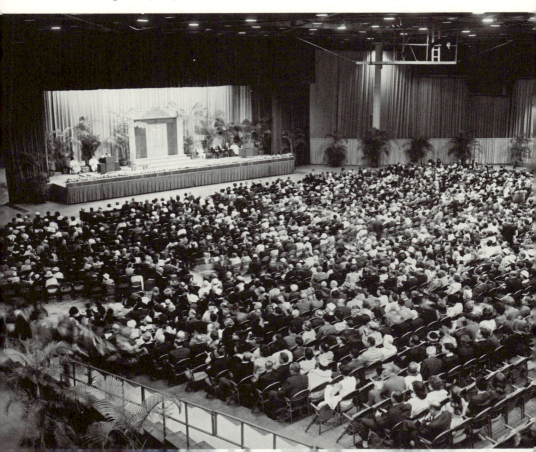

confirmation services at the Temple. This problem necessarily gave rise to the possibility of erecting a sanctuary large enough for High Holy Days services.

The death of Rabbi Zwitman started the search for a new spiritual leader. The choice fell upon Joseph R. Narot, who arrived in August 1950. He had visited the city in April, but his departure from his post in Atlantic City, New Jersey, where he had served ten years, was delayed by a mission to Israel for that congregation. He went to report on conditions in Israel so that the congregation could be guided in decisions regarding moral and material support to that country.

Narot brought to the new post positive notions of leadership that have had a powerful effect on the Temple and its programs. His concept of a strong role for the rabbi does not imply autocracy but does mean partnership. He began by asking and receiving permission to participate in all deliberations of the board except those affecting himself. The professional staff had grown to include assistant rabbis, a cantor-education director, an administrative director, and an administrative assistant; and, these individuals have been drawn into a team that works closely with the senior rabbi. Significantly, they frequently lunch together where "shop talk" and informal discussion of Temple affairs keep them in close touch with each other. The Temple gave Rabbi Narot a life contract effective August 1, 1963. This step was much debated since it did not prove entirely satisfactory in Rabbi Kaplan's case. Reassuring the rabbi about his tenure in the manner of tenure for teachers is considered desirable, and "for life" in this case really means until retirement, for which provisions are also made. Of course, the possibility of renegotiating the terms of the contract also exists.

The story of Temple Israel since 1950 belongs largely to Joseph R. Narot, the assistants and the staff which he directs, and the lay leadership. The first addition to staff, Cantor Bornstein in 1952, and his work in music and religious education will be discussed in chapter eleven. Edward Cohen joined the team in 1957 as administrative director, responsible for management of properties, overseeing the budget, and implementing decisions by the board. The significant fact is his status as a fully participating member of the professional team. His name appears frequently as acting secretary at Temple board and other meetings.

The office of administrative director evolved out of a lengthy development. At the time of his appointment special provisions were made so that he would in no way replace Janet H. (Mrs. Louis) Zeientz, known by everyone as Jennie, who began serving the Temple in various secretarial ways from the time she and her husband helped to organize the congregation. From 1934 to 1960 she held the position of Temple secretary. She lived until July 22, 1964. Louis Zeientz became president of the congregation in 1926 and remained active in its affairs until his death in 1955. At the annual meeting of the congregation in May 1944, President Herman Wall described Mrs. Zeientz as "the most important personality in Temple Israel . . . for Jennie is not only our Executive Secretary, but our Telephone Operator, Assistant Rabbi, Caretaker and Manager of the whole business."

The first director of administration was Allen I. Freehling, a member of a third generation Reform family. He graduated from the University of Miami in 1953. Before beginning work at

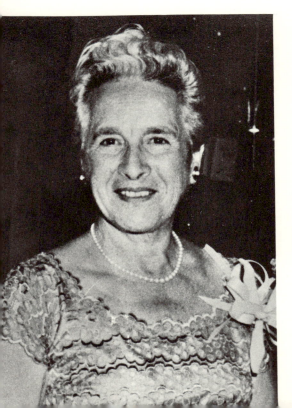

Janet H. "Jennie" (Mrs. Louis) Zeientz, pictured at the dinner honoring her at the time of her retirement

the Temple he worked as administrative assistant to President Jay F. W. Pearson at the University of Miami and in public relations for Stylaneze Furniture Company. After serving for a time at Temple Israel, he moved to Temple Emanu El, Miami Beach, in the same capacity. He resigned in 1962 to begin study for the rabbinate at Hebrew Union College, where he was ordained in 1967. He is now associate rabbi at the Collingwood Avenue Temple in Toledo, Ohio. The office had completed the evolution into a full-time job with enough salary and status for the holder to become a "member of the team" when Edward Cohen arrived in 1957.

Edward Cohen belies the image likely to be associated with his title. He is not by training or experience the professional manager type; his background is in journalism, labor organization, and politics in New Jersey. He came to Miami in 1957 to be employed by one of the newspapers, but he decided instead to take the position at Temple Israel. He is responsible for buildings and grounds, accounts and records, but he has developed a competent office staff and a maintenance crew to look after details in those areas. He is involved in budget making and management and in fund raising, all of which are clearly associated with his title, but he is much more. He participates in many aspects of Temple life and activity. He may work with a home study and discussion group as a leader or as a resource person in his area of competence. Occasionally he moderates the discussion in one of the lecture series or speaks to a class in the religious school. In the Jewish community he works in the Greater Miami Federation, speaks at other synagogues and secular organizations, and consults with other congregations on administrative matters. He is on the Speakers Bureau for Israel Relief and on the executive committee of the local federation of the Union of American Hebrew Congregations. He actively participates in politics, having won election as a Democratic County Committeeman, writes a weekly column of comment for *The Jewish Floridian,* and lectures occasionally to human relations classes at the University of Miami.

Tribute should, of course, be paid to other workers in the

earlier days before jobs became salaried and professional. Mentioning some of them should not be interpreted as intentionally ignoring others perhaps even more deserving of recognition. These workers and others like them demonstrate what keeps such institutions going in their formative years. For example, Mrs. Herman Homa, ignoring her own role of long service, reminisced about Adolph and Rose Wertheimer. "Adolph, when Holy Days came, saw that people paid their dues. Adolph went after you. If you didn't pay them in the Sisterhood, Jennie Zeientz went after you. But Adolph was the financial secretary for years, and he was the life of the Temple for many, many years. Rose Wertheimer was the house chairman and everything was in order. She kept that kitchen in order; if you wanted to have a card party or anything else, you brought back anything you borrowed. She checked out everything." In May 1950 at the annual meeting, Adolph made the dinner arrangements for the 358 persons present, the fifteenth time he had done so. He also blew the shofar at High Holy Days services. After his death, Mrs. Wertheimer presented his three ram's horns to the Temple.

In February 1956 the board authorized the employment of an assistant rabbi. Dr. Kaplan was still available for service on special occasions but could not be asked to perform continuously. The first man selected declined the offer, and Rabbi Maurice N. Eisendrath, president of UAHC, came to assist at High Holy Days services. In 1957 Rabbi Morris W. Graff came as guest rabbi and assisted at the services. At the time he did not wish a full duty assignment. In 1958, the search for an assistant, but specifically not excluding Graff from consideration, continued. In January 1959, Elijah Palnick came for an interview and subsequently accepted the post to begin in July. Before the year was out, however, he resigned effective July 1, 1960. In December 1958 Rabbi Graff became director of adult education with particular responsibility for the instruction of adult converts to Judaism. Upon the departure of Palnick, he became assistant rabbi at Temple Israel. He served until retirement in June 1971. Since he had no desire to have a congregation of his own again, Graff was in some respects an ideal assistant rabbi, but he also preferred a more limited assignment.

Early in 1967 a second assistant rabbi was authorized, and Steven B. Jacobs, a recent Hebrew Union College graduate, accepted the post. He was representative of the new activist approach to life with a strong appeal to youth. In 1970 he moved to his own congregation in Tarzana, near Encino, California. Barry Tabachnikoff succeeded him. When Rabbi Graff retired, Nicolas Behrmann came to fill that position. The personal lives and religious leadership of all the rabbis will be discussed in separate chapters.

As the membership has grown and the programs have been expanded, new facilities to house the activities have been added. In 1955 the Colman A. Zwitman Religious School east of the main sanctuary provided some twenty-two classrooms. Associated with it are the Dr. Jacob H. Kaplan Chapel and the Morris D. Wolfson Auditorium, also dedicated in 1955. The next major addition was the Sam C. Levenson Community House west of the Temple, between the Temple and the Miramar Elementary School, dedicated in 1961. On the first floor are the offices of the rabbis and the administrative staff, a Board Room, a Braille workshop, the Sisterhood Sewing Room, and the William and Irene Siegel Museum of Judaica. On the second floor are an auxiliary auditorium seating 300, a youth lounge, and classrooms. These rooms, together with those in the Zwitman School Building, provide thirty-four classrooms.

Biblical gardens provided by Mrs. Sam Resnick and twenty-three other contributors in 1955 added to the beauty of the Temple and aimed to inspire and attract people to the sanctuary and the religious school. The gardens were filled partly with plants with Biblical associations and partly with plants of a conventional formal garden. The gardens gave way in 1969 to a new building on the site.

The most recent, and for some the most controversial, building is the Nathan and Sophie Gumenick Chapel, dedicated Sunday, April 13, 1969. Adjoining other Temple buildings on the east, on the site of the Biblical gardens, it was designed by Kenneth Treister, who was confirmed at Temple Israel.

The chapel is a striking example of the dramatic and even radical revolution in religious architecture in the United States

Gumenick Chapel under construction, 1968

in recent decades. It is an interesting and undoubtedly significant commentary on the American social scene that the most radical changes in architecture have been in the two institutions commonly regarded as the most conservative—banks and churches. The chapel reaffirms Rabbi Narot's faith in the reemergence of Miami's downtown area as the heart of the metropolis. It further commits Temple Israel to remain in the heart of the city and contribute to its beauty by its own buildings.

The chapel has been characterized variously. Some perplexed and shocked by the unusual design referred to it in somewhat derisive terms as the concrete-colored bulge on Northeast Nineteenth Street, a big stone igloo with holes chopped in it, a flintstone monstrosity, and Joe's Cave. The architect and his supporters explain that they have transformed religious architecture into modern forms and ancient symbols have been presented in contemporary materials and forms. Examples are Sabbath inscribed on candelabra, a bust of Moses, a modern burning bush, and a Menorah lamp burning outside a temple. Another feature of the chapel are the eleven, three dimensional, stained-glass windows made for it in Belgium. The chapel certainly personifies the experiment in Reform Judaism which the congregation is sometimes called. Some profess to detect an undercurrent of pride in the protest. The Morris D. Wolfson Auditorium to the north of the 300-seat chapel makes possible dinners, receptions, and other social events associated with Temple activities.

A Temple Israel Master Plan, originally projected for 1972 as part of the golden anniversary celebration at a cost of some four million dollars, was made by Pancoast, Ferendino, and Grafton, architects, known for their interest in urban planning. It centers around a two-thousand-seat sanctuary to be constructed between the new chapel and the street to the east, now occupied by a service facility of McGahey Motors. It will also house the Joseph R. Narot Center for Advanced Jewish Studies. This plan includes a museum and art gallery to exhibit the present collection of almost 200 Jewish ceremonial objects and artifacts and space for additions to it. There will be a closely related museum office, preparation area, and administrative suite. The present 6,000 volumes of Judaica in the Temple Library will be expanded to an estimated 15,000 and housed in larger quarters. Seminar halls for visiting and resident students and scholars will also be provided.

The library is one of the prized features of the Temple program. In its modern form it originated in 1944 when Reba Engler (Mrs. Leonard) Epstein pledged an initial $500 as a memorial to her husband who had recently died during his term as president of the congregation. At the time the library consisted of a few books in a broom closet under a stairway in Kaplan Hall. It then became the Leonard Epstein Memorial Library with two rooms assigned to it and a Library Board to administer it. It is now usually referred to as the Temple Israel Library, but a plaque beneath a photograph of Leonard Epstein states that it was dedicated to him. Contributions soon provided chairs, tables, and shelving, and President Max Orovitz reported in May 1945 that physical arrangements for the library were ready.

Progress at building the collection was relatively slow at first. The library was dependent mostly upon contributions and volunteer help, but it has had continuously improving support ever since. Trudy Berlin introduced professional library practices. Annette (Mrs. Sidney) Smith was a gifted nonprofessional volunteer with a love of books. The greatest boon to the library was Max Meisel, a bibliographer and librarian and president of the congregation who devoted much time and attention to it. By the time Beatrice T. (Mrs. David) Muskat became librarian in 1961 the collection was about 1,500 volumes. It has had regular budget support from the Temple since that time. This library is largely for Temple members. The greater part of the holdings are in English. The older and larger library of the Bureau of Jewish Education is trilingual, Hebrew and Yiddish as well as English, to serve the needs of all the synagogues in the Greater Miami area.

In March 1966, the Temple dedicated the Elias Salzburg Music Library, given by Mr. and Mrs. Howard Klivans in honor

Four buildings in the Temple Israel complex. Left to right: The Sam C. Levenson Community House, the main sanctuary, the Colman A. Zwitman Religious School, and the Gumenick Chapel with the Morris D. Wolfson Auditorium to the rear.

of Mrs. Klivans' mother. The expansion of the music library, the museum of Judaica, and the general library will be at the heart of the Joseph R. Narot Center for Advanced Jewish Studies.

Land has been acquired for the projected expansion of buildings and parking space. The paved parking area directly across the street from the existing buildings is leased from the county until the year 2002. The area east of that to the street has been acquired from the City of Miami. Overflow parking is permitted on the school property west of the paved parking lot. An overhead passage with escalators in the parking lot will lead directly into the new sanctuary. The final acquisition is the purchase of land for the relocation of the McGahey Motor Company maintenance and repair facility which is now located east of the Gumenick Chapel. The new sanctuary is planned for that area.

The master plan for the development of the complex of buildings on Northeast Nineteenth Street has been suspended for the time being. At the Friday evening service on January 28, 1972, honoring founders and pioneers, President Martin Fine announced a new order of priorities and suggested new directions. A religious education center will be developed in the southwest section of Greater Miami to reach children in that growing area who cannot easily make the trip to the central school at the sanctuary. This is something of a compromise with the purpose to remain in the central city; but, it is also perhaps a necessary step in the realization of that purpose.

In recognition of the growing importance of the retreat for Temple youth activities, the congregation has purchased a fifteen acre site at 25001 Southwest 167 Avenue, a location that will reduce the logistical problems of getting away for a weekend of cultural isolation and religious-social activities. A generous donation of the down payment by the family of the late Sidney Meyer made possible the purchase of the retreat, now named the Sidney and Zenia Meyer Religious Retreat.

Part of the plan to remain in the central city because of its central geographic location is to make the facilities of the Temple available as a community center. The most important regular user of the Temple facilities is the Dade County Board

Retreat site at 25001 Southwest 167 Avenue looking northwest from pavilion area

of Public Instruction whose offices for staff development are on the school property across the street. Meetings of from thirty to several hundred persons may be held at any time during the week. The advantage to the school board is obvious. During the week it has ample space for parking for meetings of any size up to 700 persons, and another 400 can meet in another auditorium at the same time. A payment of $10,000 a year covers the costs of maintenance and utilities.

Adon Taft, religious editor for *The Miami Herald,* described the activities for a month in the fall of 1969. A mental health fair attracted one thousand people. Between November 3 and 6, the 300 member Council for the Continuing Education for Women was in session. The Interfaith Agency for Social Justice held a meeting, as did the Greater Miami Rabbinical Association and the visiting teachers of Dade County. In the next week, the Federation of Temple Youth held two days of sessions, and the

Anti-Defamation League of B'nai B'rith met the third day. Others holding meetings were the American Jewish Committee, The Board of Jewish Vocational Services, and the Dade County Citizens Safety Council. In the third week users were the Girl Scout Council of Tropical Florida, Brandeis University Women, and the Middle East Committee of the Greater Miami Jewish Federation. In the fourth week a downtown Interfaith Thanksgiving Service featuring the U.S. Air Force Academy's choir was held in the sanctuary.

Temple facilities are used every school day by the Head Start program, which has used six classrooms since 1966, and by Miami-Dade Junior College, which offered a credit course in Jewish culture at the Temple in the 1972 spring term.

Chairman E. Albert Pallot of the Miami City Beautification Committee presenting the committee's annual award to Rabbi Narot for Temple Israel's contribution to city beautification, March 1969. Alfred Browning Parker is on the left and John D. Pennekamp is on the right.

6/Rabbi Jacob H. Kaplan and the Depression Years, 1926-1941

Only three rabbis, Jacob H. Kaplan, Colman A. Zwitman, and Joseph R. Narot have had long enough tenure as spiritual leaders at Temple Israel to significantly and measurably influence its development. A review of the leadership of each will demonstrate the nature and importance of the office and how much it reflects the personality of the man himself.

When Rabbi Jacob H. Kaplan came to Temple Israel in 1926, he was just over fifty years of age and a man of considerable experience, having served several congregations. The lay leadership, on the other hand, had only a few years of leadership experience. The congregation was already beginning to feel the strain of a depression that was to become worse, and they faced a building program that was to tax their resources. Dr. Kaplan wished to be excluded from a leading role in management. He strongly disliked fund raising and felt it should never be directly associated with worship services. In a time of financial stringency this attitude was sometimes frustrating to the lay leaders. He did ask for and receive permission to make his monthly reports to the board in person so that any questions raised might be discussed, but after his presentation and a question period he retired from the meeting. He regularly reported his activities to the board and asked approval for anything beyond his purely spiritual duties. Rabbi Zwitman followed essentially the same practice. Rabbi Narot, on the other hand, asked for and received permission to be present at all board meetings except when he himself was the subject of discussion and action. He has been a fully participating partner.

Dr. Kaplan had a deep and wide interest in interfaith activities in the Miami community and in the state, but he also felt his responsibilities to his coreligionists and congregants. He organized both the state and the Greater Miami rabbinical associations and served them as president. His rabbinical colleagues selected him to represent them in a short course at the University of Florida for ministers in April 1938. Some of his congre-

Rabbi Jacob H. Kaplan, with Mrs. Kaplan at his right, speaking at ground-breaking ceremonies in 1927. Other adults in the photograph are from left to right: Harry Simons, Pearl (Mrs. Nat) Roth (Nat Roth behind her), Tilly Liebovit (Lee), Norman Mirsky, and Morris Plant. Children pictured left to right are Barbara Homa and Marian Fried.

gants felt at times that he was neglecting them for activity in the wider field. He was a Mason, an Elk, and a sixty-six-year Shriner.

Jacob Hyman Kaplan was born at Adelman, in Posen Province, Germany, on December 26, 1874. At seven he came with his parents and his sister, Millie, to Buffalo, New York. His mother and his sister, unable to adjust to the new life, returned to Germany after one year but came back to America at about the time Jacob was going to the seminary. His father first sent him to business school but readily yielded to his son's wish to enter the rabbinate. At nineteen, Jacob, whose whole experience had been Orthodox, saw his first Reform service and found it to his liking. His Orthodox father yielded in this regard also and accompanied his son to Cincinnati when Jacob entered Hebrew Union College, from which he graduated in 1902. His college studies were interrupted for a year during which he went to Denver, Colorado, for his health. During that stay he began some studies at the University of Denver which permitted him to earn the Ph.D. in philosophy there in 1906; his dissertation was on the "Psychology of Prophecy."

His first temple was in Albuquerque, New Mexico, where his sister Millie made a home for him and acted as his hostess until he married Adele Hoffman in Selma, Alabama, in 1907. His stay in Albuquerque revealed some of his tendencies. With a Christian minister he started a newspaper, *The Barbarian,* which championed the rights of the underprivileged. An article defending the civil and social rights of blacks which the young rabbi wrote made his position almost untenable. After serving briefly in Jackson, Mississippi, he was at Selma, Alabama, from 1906 to 1911, after which he went to Terre Haute, Indiana, from 1911 to 1913. His final assignment before coming to Miami was at Israel Temple, usually referred to as the Reading Road Temple, in Cincinnati. He exhibited again his strong ecumenical spirit in Cincinnati, a center of opposition to Zionism, by opening his pulpit to speakers on Zionism. The question was producing great controversy in American Judaism at times, and Kaplan, though his commitment to Reform was extreme in some respects, gave more support than most Reform Jews to Zionism. He managed, however, to avoid quarreling over the issue and remained on good terms with people of all shades of opinion. One of his lecturers on Zionism was the "peoples' lawyer," Louis D. Brandeis. A year after his appearance in Kaplan's pulpit, Brandeis was named to the U.S. Supreme Court by President Woodrow Wilson.

At Temple Israel Rabbi Kaplan continued to bring in noted speakers. In 1936 they included such notables as Rabbi Stephen S. Wise and Will Durant. In fact, he opened his pulpit to such a variety of people and subjects that the board took action to require the approval

In World War I Rabbi Kaplan, pictured here with Mrs. Kaplan in 1917, served as a chaplain at Camp Merritt, New Jersey.

of the president if anyone outside the rabbinate was to be invited.

In his annual report in 1928 he wrote, "A Reform Jewish Temple is a three-fold House of God. It is a House of Prayer, a House of Study, and a House of Social Intercourse. The Rabbi is not a pastor who visits his members to pray with them. The Rabbi's chief work is to teach, to teach in the Temple and to inspire, to teach in the classroom, that the members may have an adequate conception of the beauty and sublimity of our religion, and that the world may know the meaning of Reform in Jewish life." He argued that Reform Jews must know Judaism in order to study how to reform it. In September 1928 the board approved of his conducting an open forum in the main auditorium on Sunday mornings, a class in Bible study Sunday evenings, and a class in Judaism at a time to be selected by him. Mrs. Kaplan at times shared with him the direction of religious education until Rabbi Zwitman came to be assistant rabbi and take over the religious school.

The University of Miami afforded Dr. Kaplan the opportunity to pursue his love of teaching and his interest in philosophy. He taught philosophy at the university from 1930 to 1945 except for three years. He received no salary but accepted fifty dollars a month for expenses. The histories of other major

Dr. Kaplan, professor of philosophy, with his colleagues on the University of Miami faculty. Seated left to right: Dr. Kaplan and Dr. William H. McMaster, professor of religion. Standing left to right are the members of the history department: Dr. Paul Eckel, Dr. Charlton W. Tebeau, Dr. Harold E. Briggs (chairman), Dr. H. Franklin Williams, and Dr. Robert E. McNicoll.

Miami institutions parallel that of Temple Israel, for example, the University of Miami. The collapse of the real estate boom after 1925 and the same hurricane that greeted Dr. Kaplan brought collapse to the splendid plans and generous promises of financial support for a university in the burgeoning metropolis. After the storm in September 1926 the university abandoned its one unfinished building and opened in another unfinished structure intended for a hotel; the university did not complete the building on the original campus until twenty years later. Then the university entered a period of unprecedented growth roughly comparable to that of Temple Israel and the entire Greater Miami community.

Temple Israel members have also been associated with the University of Miami and other educational institutions. Leonard L. Abess, Baron de Hirsch Meyer, Max Orovitz, and Arthur A. Ungar have served on the board of trustees of the university, Orovitz as chairman of the executive committee. Julian I. Weinkle headed the Citizens Board for the university for two years. Mitchell Wolfson has been chairman of the Board of Trustees of Miami-Dade Junior College since the college was organized. William Lehman and Jack Gordon have served on the Dade County Board of Public Instruction, Lehman as chairman.

The late Harry Simonhoff aptly characterized Dr. Kaplan as a liberal humanist. Simonhoff felt that Kaplan's emphasis on liberal principles drew him to Reform Judaism. In fact, one of Dr. Kaplan's most prominent congregants, Max Orovitz, expressed the view that the pendulum swung so far that Reform Judaism at Temple Israel took on much of the nature of a Christian church. Rabbi Kaplan did represent some of the reactions to Orthodoxy that opposed such traditions as a cantor, bar mitzvah, vestments for the clergy, any suggestion that the choir or any other aspect of the service should be exclusively Jewish, or anything but limited use of the Hebrew language. To the consternation of many members of the board and the congregation, he once preached a sermon on humanism at a New Year service. It was charged that he did so because some persons outside the Temple had expressed interest in it.

Rabbi Jacob H. Kaplan [89]

Dr. Kaplan got along well with all denominations of Christians, but he had a special place in his affections for Unitarians. He helped organize the First Unitarian Church in Miami, donated $200 from his slender resources, and helped them find a meeting place. He was quoted as saying, "I prefer to serve synagogues where there is a Unitarian Church because the institution has a clearing effect upon the community."

On May 19, 1936, he reported to the board that he had helped to organize a Miami Round Table of the National Conference of Christians and Jews (NCCJ) for the purpose of creating better relations between Protestants, Catholics, and Jews. Reorganized some years later under the more direct sponsorship of the NCCJ, the Miami Round Table became a continuing feature of local radio programming.

In the same report he wrote: "As an ambassador to the community for Temple Israel, which a Reform Rabbi has to be, I have attended at least 25 to 30 meetings for Jewish interests and twelve for civic interest. I have lectured on many occasions, whenever and wherever invited." After the 1935 Labor Day hurricane he joined a Catholic priest and a Christian minister and spent a day conducting funerals for storm victims on the islands. In 1937 he repeated the list of activities as if responding to criticism and asked the board if he should continue. When Rabbi Zwitman came as his assistant, Kaplan felt released to more interfaith activity, saying that the younger man could organize youth groups in the congregation. To the end of his active career he remained interested and involved in the greater world around him. In July 1948 he was reporting to the Temple board his commitment to speak for the United World Federalists, Inc., a world peace movement. In 1947 he published *Sparks From a Mental Anvil,* a collection of his axiomatic sayings on a wide variety of topics. He had earlier, in 1908, published *The Psychology of Prophesy* based upon his doctoral dissertation. He also started *Jewish Unity,* a weekly that evolved into *The Jewish Floridian,* published by the Shochet family.

Rabbi Kaplan died January 6, 1965, shortly after the celebration of his ninetieth birthday, revered and venerated by Jew and non-Jew alike. Mrs. Kaplan had died on January 13, 1956. A cousin, Maurice Kohen and his wife, Anne, then moved in with Dr. Kaplan to make a home for him until his death nine years later.

Mrs. Herman I. Homa expressed it very well when she said: "Well, Rabbi Kaplan came and he was a joy to everybody. Everybody loved him and he had the sweetest nature of any man that I have known in the rabbinate. He knew what he wanted to do. . . . He organized the women and he got everybody to working and he really made our Temple what it was until later years, until he got too old." Henry Wolff expressed the same sentiment when he said: "He looked like a rabbi and he was highly respected in the community. . . . He gave you a feeling of dignity and reverence. . . ."

Rabbi Jacob H. Kaplan (in white) at age 85 in 1960 on the occasion of the celebration of Rabbi Joseph R. Narot's twentieth year in the rabbinate and the tenth at Temple Israel. Left to right: Rabbi Morris W. Graff, Rabbi Irving M. Lehrman (Temple Emanu El, Miami Beach), Rabbi Nathan Perilman (Temple E Manuel, New York City), Monsignor James Enright (St. Rose of Lima Roman Catholic Church, Miami), Rabbi Narot, Reverend Harold Buell (White Temple Methodist Church, Miami), and Rabbi Kaplan.

7/Rabbi Colman A. Zwitman, 1936-1949

Colman A. Zwitman came to Temple Israel as assistant rabbi in 1936, became associate rabbi two years later, and senior rabbi in 1941 when Dr. Jacob H. Kaplan retired to emeritus status. Rabbi Zwitman's tenure was interrupted from 1943 to 1946 when he served as chaplain in the U.S. Army, where he contracted a disease that cost him his life in 1949. His war experiences and his early death have greatly colored recollections of his life and work, but they should not be allowed to obscure what the record reveals before and beyond the tragic end of a promising career. The young rabbi was at Temple Israel long enough before he entered the army to have a positive impact upon the congregation and to give clearly recognizable new direction by his leadership. This leadership was especially dynamic since he was able to effect changes even though he came as assistant rabbi and lived throughout his tenure, even after he became the senior rabbi, somewhat in the shadow of Rabbi Kaplan. Happily, Dr. Kaplan seems to have been willing that the younger man have a relatively free hand.

After Zwitman's death one member of the congregation said, "Zwitman had something going for him. I don't know what it was." He had youth; he was only twenty-six when he came to Miami. He had a good singing voice, and many people, members and nonmembers, came to hear him sing or chant parts of the ritual. Members recall particularly the seder, Kol Nidre, and the kiddush. His chanting undoubtedly paved the way for the eventual employment of a cantor at Temple Israel.

He was an effective speaker and was soon in demand locally and throughout the state. On May 4, 1937, he appeared at Fort Lauderdale where the Jewish community was meeting at City Hall to begin steps to establish a congregation. In November the board approved his trip to Gainesville to speak to Jewish students at the University of Florida and his return by way of Orlando and Lakeland to speak to Jewish groups there. On July 5, 1939, he spoke at a service in the Temple of Religion at the New York World's Fair at which the choir of Temple Beth-El of Great Neck, Long Island, sang a twilight concert. Other engagements called him to school commencements and service clubs. In September 1940 he became adviser to students in the Hillel Chapter at the University of Miami. In the same year he became a member of the Miami Round Table Radio Forum, serving

The clerical trio on the interfaith radio program sponsored by the National Conference of Christians and Jews on Saturday evenings, circa 1942. Left to right: Father Florence Sullivan, Dr. H. Franklin Williams (moderator), Reverend Roger Squire, and Rabbi Colman A. Zwitman.

with Reverend Roger Squire of Rader Memorial Methodist Church and Father Florence Sullivan of Gesu Catholic Church. Radio was as important at that time as television is today, and through that medium he carried the message of Judaism and brotherhood to a wide audience. Many of those persons who joined Temple Israel during Rabbi Zwitman's tenure recall that his singing, his involvement with their children in the religious school, his preaching, and his personality were important reasons for their attraction to Temple Israel. The religious school, which is discussed in chapter nine, was one of his principal concerns from the time of his arrival.

Colman A. Zwitman was born in Russia on May 15, 1910. His parents fled with him and his brother, Nathan, to Palestine. The family later migrated to New York, where a daughter was born, but the father returned to Israel after the mother's death. From his parents Colman inherited a deep interest in learning. His father was very much the scholar, and his mother's skill as a linguist made it possible for her to contribute substantially to the family's income. The father was less practical. Colman studied at New York and Columbia universities and at Hebrew Teachers College. He prepared for the rabbinate at the Jewish Institute of Religion founded by Rabbi Stephen S. Wise in New York. Later this eastern branch of American Reform Judaism was affiliated with the midwestern branch at Hebrew Union College (HUC) in Cincinnati, with which Temple Israel has previously been closely associated. His experience was limited to that of the student rabbi doing visiting duty in several congregations and to a brief tenure in Bluefield, West Virginia, from which he was released to come to Miami.

He also represented a return to more form and ritual in the service in a congregation that seemed determined to prove its Reformism by rejecting all symbols of Orthodoxy. For example, at a board meeting on September 8, 1936, a motion to have rabbis wear white suits was tabled. There must have been some protest about Zwitman's practices. The Ritual Committee, a sort of vigilance committee on such matters, reported to the board that "Rabbi Zwitman had conducted services with the accepted decorum and dignity of a Reform Temple. Yet he has always injected enough of traditional Judaism to gladden the hearts of those to whom it was pleasing."

One congregant who obviously approved Zwitman's unobtrusive introduction of more ritual in the ceremony said that Zwitman was really Orthodox at heart. Certainly he had all the educational qualifications. Dr. Sidney L. Besvinick recalls that one Saturday morning Rabbi Zwitman came to Beth Jacob, then a small Orthodox synagogue on South Beach. He read and chanted the ritual in Hebrew and then delivered a sermon in beautiful Yiddish. Intellectually he was on the side of Reform and did not let ritual and form dominate his approach.

In October 1948 when the two Reform seminaries, Hebrew Union College and the Jewish Institute of Religion, joined forces, Zwitman was invited to give the principal address at the opening of the school year in New York City. Present on the occasion were Dr. Nelson Glueck, newly elected president of HUC and the associated Jewish Institute of Religion, and the emeritus presidents of the two organizations, Dr. Julian Morgenstern and Dr. Stephen S. Wise. Zwitman continued his service to the affiliated institutions, receiving the grateful thanks of the presidents of HUC and the UAHC, Union of American Hebrew Congregations, when he rallied the Miami Jewry to support the combined appeal for those two institutions of Reform Judaism early in 1948.

Rabbi Zwitman's years in the army, 1943-46, were busy indeed. A grateful civilian living near Fort Monmouth, New Jersey, where he was first stationed, wrote to Temple Israel on April 20, 1945, to express his gratitude. The writer was one of ninety-two Jewish families living in a government housing project, Alfred Vail Homes, near the fort. A chapel was available, and the Catholics and Protestants used it, but the Jews could not find a rabbi to officiate at services. When they took their problem to the chief of army personnel at Fort Monmouth, he replied that Chaplain Zwitman was the only rabbi on the post and that he was already far too busy. In addition to being responsible for Fort Monmouth, he was taking care of its sub-posts, hospitals, and bivouac areas. The anxious civilian group then took their problem to the chaplain. They discovered that on Friday he was doing a service for the Officer Candidate School at four in the afternoon, for the guardhouse at five, for the hospital at six, and for the post in the post chapel at 8:15. He could, he said, do one for the Vail Homes group at seven. When he was transferred in 1945, the civic organizations of three northern New Jersey communities gave a testimonial for the chaplain.

En route to his new assignment in the Philippines, the commander of the U.S.S. *Osage* reported on September 11, 1945, that Captain Zwitman had arrived on board on August 27, and that as senior army chaplain aboard he was assigned to assist the ship's chaplain in the performance of chaplain's duties for the army personnel. In addition to performing religious services for Jewish soldiers, he had arranged for a Catholic rosary service and a service for Mormons led by a layman, he had coordinated the activities of three other chaplains, and he had taken part in Protestant religious and song services.

When the Japanese took over the city of Manila in 1944,

Rabbi Zwitman in uniform during World War II

they converted the only synagogue into an ammunition
dump. When they evacuated
the city the next year, they
blew up the ammunition, de-
stroying the building. In the
ruins of the synagogue Rabbi
Zwitman led a memorial service for Americans of all faiths
who had fallen in the Philippines. Those present pledged
themselves to rebuild the synagogue as a living memorial to
their comrades. In the Philippines he also contracted the
liver ailment that later cost
him his life on December 23,
1949. President Harry S. Tru-
man awarded Chaplain Zwitman a captain's commission in
the U.S. Army Reserves, the
first such commission given to
a Jewish chaplain who had
served in World War II.

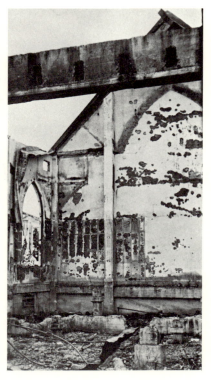

Bombed synagogue, Manila, 1944

In the summer of 1946 he resumed his full schedule of duties
at Temple Israel. If anything, he expanded the scope of his
interest and work. In 1947 he took public issue with a Protestant minister in Miami who appeared to him to condone anti-
Semitism in the name of free speech in a Columbus Day sermon. Rabbi Zwitman asked for a full text of the sermon since
he had seen only three paragraphs quoted in *The Miami Herald*.
He invited the minister's congregation to come to Temple Israel
on Friday, October 24, to hear a Jewish rabbi's answer and
offered his pulpit to the minister the following Friday night to
reply. Zwitman conceded that anti-Semites have a right to criti-
cize anyone they wish, but they do not have the right to incite
to evil action and to riot. He insisted also that anti-Semite

Rabbi Colman A. Zwitman [97]

meant anti-Jew. Nothing came of the episode except an exchange of letters, but Rabbi Zwitman made his point.

In 1948 Colman Zwitman's career reached its peak in activity and recognition. In addition to the work for the combined appeal mentioned earlier, Frank Weil, president of the National Jewish Welfare Board, honored Zwitman with a certificate from the Division of Religious Activities for his service to American and World Jewry. The Jewish Service Bureau of Miami presented him with a certificate of merit for his effort in obtaining the largest number of new members for the organization. At the annual convention of the UAHC in Boston he was awarded a plaque for his outstanding achievement and for forwarding the cause of Reform Judaism in America. The National Conference of Christians and Jews expressed its deep appreciation to the rabbi for his superior assistance to the promotion of American brotherhood. Finally, early in 1949, the selection committee chose him as Miami's Outstanding Citizen for 1948. Specifically mentioned were his religious work, his part in the Freedom Train ceremonies for which he had written the script used in the religious pageant in Miami, and for promoting the welfare of all faiths.

The ravages of the disease he had contracted during his military service were beginning to wear him down and rob him of the energy to carry on a full schedule of activity. He continued to meet his congregation for the Friday evening service, seemingly able to rise above his affliction for that occasion. To the younger people who protested the unfairness of his illness and impending death, he explained it as God's way of calling attention to the evil of war. He died on December 24, 1949, survived by his wife, Lenore, and two sons, Joseph and Michael.

Colman Zwitman's death at thirty-nine years of age ended the career of one of American Reform Judaism's most able practitioners and advocates. In the congregation, in the community, and in the nation he was already making his mark indelibly, and he would not soon be forgotten. The dedication at Temple Israel of the Colman A. Zwitman Religious School Building five years after his death is but one mark of that recognition.

8/Joseph R. Narot:
Rabbi in Command,
1950-1972

The leadership of Dr. Joseph R. Narot at Temple Israel covers almost half of the life of the congregation. He arrived in Miami in 1950 after serving a relatively small congregation in a small Jewish community in Atlantic City, New Jersey. He left one resort community to go to another, but there the similarity in the communities ended. Greater Miami was already caught up in a population explosion that would soon transform it into a teeming metropolis at the hub of some two million people in a three-county area and that would bring to it the sixth largest number of Jews in the United States. In the Miami area Rabbi Narot was to find an outlet for all the energy, concern, and ability that he possessed. That neither he nor the congregation of Temple Israel guessed where his leadership might lead them is abundantly clear. The lay leadership was dynamic in a community overflowing with vitality, but the spiritual leader of Temple Israel was to be the architect of much that occurred in his congregation.

Joseph R. Narot was born in a little town near Vilna in Lithuania on April 24, 1913. The family came to the United States in 1920 and settled in Warren, Ohio, a town almost as limited in outlook as the one from which he had come. His upbringing was Orthodox, and his mind was steeped in the lore of Hebrew language and Judaism. It is perhaps significant that his mother thought the nutritional needs of a growing boy might justify an occasional violation of strict dietary law. Only when the family moved to Cleveland did the eighteen-year-old Joseph discover Reform Judaism. There, two great rabbis, Alba Hillel Silver and Barnett Brickner, did much to confirm his commitment to Reform. He has continued to be a student of Judaism and a foremost interpreter of Reform ideas and practices in his sermons and published writings. He earned his baccalaureate degree at Western Reserve University at Cleveland, and with it election to Phi Beta Kappa. He then entered Hebrew Union College in Cincinnati, where he graduated and was ordained a rabbi in 1940. Six years later he earned the degree Doctor of Hebrew Letters at the same institution. In 1965, in recognition of his continuing study and writing in the field of Reform Judaism, his alma mater awarded him the honorary degree Doctor of Divinity.

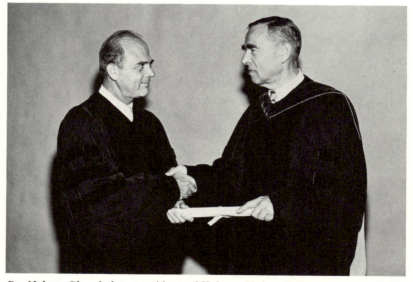

Dr. Nelson Glueck, late president of Hebrew Union College, presents Rabbi Narot with the honorary degree of Doctor of Divinity, 1965.

In Atlantic City Rabbi Narot showed some of the same interests that were to hold his attention in Miami. He served on the State Board of the New Jersey Mental Hygiene Society and as vice-president of the Atlantic County Mental Hygiene Society. His continuing interest in problems of mental health, his own and those he might be called upon to counsel, led him to undergo psychoanalysis over a considerable period of time. He was a member of Rotary Club when he came to Miami, but found regular attendance increasingly difficult. When he spoke to the downtown Miami club, he took the opportunity to chide his fellows about their membership in country clubs that excluded himself and other Jews. In Atlantic City he had also served on the City Hospital Board, the Community Chest, and the Boy Scout Council. He did not, as do some rabbis, shun fund raising; he served three years as chairman of the United Jewish Appeal.

His activities in behalf of Reform Judaism have won for him national recognition. He returned to Hebrew Union College in 1960 to deliver a series of lectures in homiletics. He served on the Executive Board of the Central Conference of American Rabbis, the national organization of Reform rabbis. His concern about the place of ritual and form in religious ceremony, his belief that it should remain a means to enrichment of religious experience rather than a rite which is an end in itself, earned for him the Chairmanship of the Liturgy Committee of the Central Conference of American Rabbis from 1965 to 1969. Since 1968 he has been a member of the National Board of the Union of American Hebrew Congregations.

Rabbi Narot has wide-ranging interests, and he manages to keep himself and his congregation abreast of what is going on in many areas. He thinks of himself primarily as a preacher. At this he is superbly effective. Nearly five thousand persons came to hear his High Holy Days sermons in September 1971 at the Miami Beach Convention Hall. Most of those attending were affiliated with Temple Israel, but some of them, as is quite customary, chose this one occasion to renew their association with Jews and Judaism. One member wrote in 1969, "How ironic it is, with all of the emphasis we put on the importance

Rabbi Joseph R. Narot [101]

Rabbi Joseph Narot and Cantor Bornstein in service at Miami Beach Convention Hall, 1969. Seated behind Rabbi Narot are, left to right, Rabbi Morris W. Graff, Sam C. Levenson, and William D. Singer.

of atmosphere that the first truly meaningful religious experience of my life should take place in the Miami Beach Convention Hall. Tonight I was able to reach out with my intellect and my feelings and touch my religious core. . . . "

The themes of most of his sermons are entirely contemporary, but the content is deeply rooted in Hebrew scriptures, history, and tradition. He aims to show that the teachings of ancient Judaism are universal, that they provide a viable approach to questions and problems of the day. It is here in his approach that he interprets Reform principles to demonstrate a rational, changing, adaptable religion, as vital today as ever, an old religion in new forms. If the members of the Temple Israel congregation hope to be soothed and reassured and made comfortable by his preachments, they are likely to be disappointed. He preaches fervently the beauty and the vitality and the contemporaneousness of the ancient faith. At the same time he is likely to jolt them out of any complacency they might feel; to tell them there is work to be done; to call them to arms against ignorance, superstition, hypocrisy, prejudice, discrimination, social injustice, and violence; and to reaffirm their faith in the dignity and worth of the human individual.

Dr. Narot is deeply concerned about religious education. He agrees with Reform Judaism, generally, that the secular school is the place for secular education. At the same time he believes with most Jews that the future of Judaism depends on education in what the faith has to offer. Religious education is an integral part of any Jewish organization. Rabbi Narot and Cantor-Educational Director Jacob Bornstein have made the educational program at Temple Israel such a vital part of the activity of the Temple that it will be given separate attention in the next chapter.

The rabbi also believes strongly that religious education must be a continuing process. It cannot, as is so frequently assumed, end when a young man has become a bar mitzvah; it must certainly continue for boys and girls through confirmation. This was one reason that Reform practice for a time discouraged, when it did not forbid, bar mitzvah, and put all the emphasis upon confirmation. But religious education was not to stop with confirmation. In fact, it should never stop. There are courses for high school students. Recently retreats at a camp sponsored by the Temple have been highly successful. The rabbi has realized his hope that Temple Israel might have its own retreat grounds to which youth groups can retire for a weekend, or longer, of recreation, music, and thought built around themes related to Judaism. Young people are formally organized in NFTY, National Federation of Temple Youth. For young married couples there is Couples Limited from which they "graduate" to the Sisterhood or the Brotherhood of the Temple. Adult education continues in the form of lectures and courses.

Rabbi Narot shares the concern of all branches of Judaism that young Jews will lose their identity when they go away to college, that they may drift away from the faith of their fathers and be assimilated into the great majority of non-Jews with whom they are thrown. Under his inspiration the Temple fol-

Rabbi Joseph R. Narot [103]

lows students to the college campus and remains in close touch with them. Students depart for college with a college kit, described by one student as "instant Judaism," largely containing literature to provide Jewish religious and cultural sustenance. At college they receive a magazine, *In Touch,* which keeps them in contact with home and with Reform Judaism at Temple Israel. When students come home for school holidays, the rabbi meets with them at a brunch and discusses any subject they choose. Other entertainment, largely social in nature, seeks to keep them allied to their home temple since they are an important part of the lifeblood of the Temple in the next generation. Recently the rabbi has visited college campuses where a large group of Temple religious school alumni attend. He meets with students from Temple Israel or telephones them individually. Support for this college program comes from the Morton A. Grant Fund of the Temple Israel Brotherhood.

Not all of this activity is unique to Temple Israel, nor is it unique to Judaism. American higher education in the beginning was largely under denominational and religious sponsorship: witness Harvard, Yale, Princeton, Columbia, and Brown, for examples. When public tax-supported and independent non-denominational schools began to appear and attract more and more students, fear became general that the hold of churches on youth would be lost. When the complete separation of church and state in schools became increasingly the law of the land, religious bodies were placed at a great disadvantage. The best they could do was to establish religious centers, usually just off campus, and offer educational, social, recreational, and religious services that would attract students. In some schools they could offer a few courses in religion that received college credit and operate dining rooms and even dormitories. Even these steps have now begun to lose their effectiveness.

The Hillel Foundation maintains campus centers to minister to the needs and hold the allegiance of Jewish students. A director, frequently a rabbi, may give all his time to this service where the Jewish student body is large enough. Temple Israel supports Hillel activities, as it does all other agencies dealing with the common interests and concerns of the Jewish community, but it goes beyond that in the effort to keep alive its identity with its own student members. The future of Temple Israel may be involved.

Within the Temple Israel membership there is some concern that the congregation has grown so large that something has been lost. Members do not and cannot know each other in the warmly human association characteristic of smaller congregations. The larger congregation can be held together only by the leadership and the program that is offered. The same members, on the other hand, to borrow the advertising slogan of a southeastern banking chain, realize that big they can do things they could not do small. This is peculiarly true in the educational program, and almost uniquely so in the program to follow students to college and university campuses.

Rabbi Narot has always insisted that his first obligation is to his own congregation, but his wide-ranging concern for human welfare and the nature of Reform Judaism as he interprets it have meant that he would be drawn into affairs outside his own temple. In *The Miami Herald,* November 25, 1965, he stated his notion of the role he should play. "But with the coming of modern times the rabbi entered into the arena of life with greater alacrity, especially in the United States. Today the rabbi in addition to teaching must also preach, take an interest in the administration of the synagogue and translate social action ideals into reality. He also serves as ambassador to the non-Jewish community. Some think the rabbi is doing too much, but the times demand that he do so." There are those who say that this particular rabbi has helped to make it so.

The rabbi's major services in the community include membership on the Dade County Community Relations Board from its organization in 1963, and then as chairman in 1966. The Metro Commission of Dade County named this board, composed of three Negroes, a Cuban, and leaders from religion, education, and business, with Bishop, now Archbishop, Coleman F. Carrol as first chairman. Narot succeeded Bishop James L. Duncan, Suffragan Bishop of the Episcopal Diocese of South Florida.

Rabbi Joseph R. Narot [105]

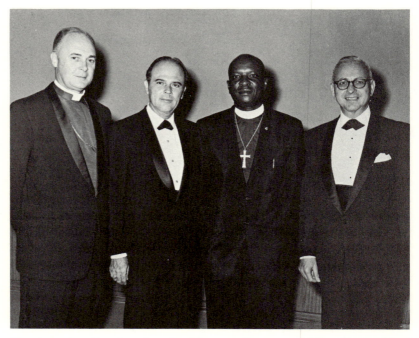

Narot receives the American Jewish committee award "For Distinguished Service in Advancing the Cause of Human Relations," 1963. Left to right: Bishop James L. Duncan, Rabbi Narot, Reverend Theodore Gibson, and Alvin Cassel.

The main thrusts during the Narot leadership were concern with integration in the schools, the adjustment of relations between Cuban and black citizens, and more open housing, all to achieve a good neighborhood concept. In 1964 the Metro Commission named him to an antipoverty task force committee to study and identify the problems of poverty in Dade County. In 1961 he succeeded Dr. H. Franklin Williams as president of the Welfare Planning Council. Its function was to coordinate the health, recreational, and welfare activities of all nonpublic agencies in the county. In 1965 the rabbi became a member of the Dade County Economic Opportunity Board. The first years of that agency were directed largely to identifying its own role and setting up machinery to achieve its goals. In 1968 Dr. Narot served as president of the Miami Chapter of the American Jewish Committee, a pioneer human relations body founded in 1906 to combat bigotry and protect the civil and religious rights of all people at home and abroad.

These public activities identify him and the temple he represents with strong advocacy of civil rights. His personal activities go even further to create such an image. At times his concern over issues of social justice and peace have spilled over into positive action. He feels that his deep concern dates back to the first years of his life in a village used by both the Germans and the Russians in an area that changed hands many times. He had had enough of violence, but he was deeply committed to non-violent and rational efforts to achieve peace and social justice. He shared the view of many of his coreligionists that Jews must participate in some such activities even if they are likely to arouse anti-Semitism. He agreed with Assistant Rabbi Steven B. Jacobs when the latter said, "The last time Jews kept still was in Nazi Germany and I'm not going to let that happen here."

Rabbi Narot became deeply concerned over the involvement of the United States in the war in Southeast Asia and became active in the protest movement against it. In 1968 he was one of thirty-seven candidates for delegates at large to the Democratic National Convention who, if they had won, were pledged to support the presidential candidacy of Senator Eugene McCarthy, at the time the foremost proponent of U.S. withdrawal from the Vietnam conflict. The rabbi explained that he was not getting into politics; he was expressing his opposition to the war and the hope that McCarthy could do something about it. Late in 1969 he spoke at a moratorium rally of students on the University of Miami campus, and again at a similar rally in Miami's Bayfront Auditorium. In November, in the midst of the antiwar activity, at the Annual Biracial Equal Opportunity Dinner, the National Urban League honored him as the Miamian who had made the most outstanding contribution to the concept of human equality in the field of human relations. In the spring of 1970 he was one of 160 Americans, and the only rabbi, at a Paris conference on the war sponsored by the American Friends Service Committee, at which both North and South Vietnam and Cambodia and Laos were represented. In May he attended a convention of clergymen and laymen concerned with Vietnam meeting in Washington, D.C., of which Dr. Martin Luther King, prior to his death by assassination, had been an organizer.

The rabbi's antiwar activity produced a wide spectrum of reactions. A few members refused to accept this role for the rabbi; others wrote in approval, while many others expressed reservations. At least one pair of students at the University of Florida thought that he was not radical enough. They recognized that there were limits beyond which he would not go, that he had not really abandoned his commitment to work "through verbal persuasion and in the arena of negotiation through personal and communal effort."

Rabbi Narot shares the concern of Jews everywhere about the security and the international status of the State of Israel. He applauds the demand of Russian Jews for ethnic and religious identity as well as unity with Jews the world over. This last may well be more important than the issue of freedom to migrate. Like his predecessors and contemporaries he has spoken out on the relation of American Jews in general to Israel and his own congregants in particular. Rabbi Zwitman in 1946 took the position that Jews who remain in America have the same opportunity and obligation to preserve Judaism. "If Jewish tradition should live," he wrote, "it would be through the efforts of the American Jew, therefore, the congregation must assume this responsibility and the Temple should be the symbol of American Jewishness."

Rabbi Narot has visited Israel five times: in 1950, 1959, 1967, 1970, and 1971. He too refuses to tie Judaism to the fate of the national state however important it may be as a living symbol of the ancient faith. In 1971, upon his return, he reminded his congregation, "We, too, are the people of Israel. . . . Only when we see ourselves in this perspective, perhaps, do we realize the significance of the task we perform in behalf of

Judaism. Only then can we appreciate that which is close at hand, which is just as dramatic, just as fascinating, and just as critical as that at great distances away."

He and other spokesmen for American Jewry fear that much Jewish interest and many resources may be diverted from America to Israel at the cost of the welfare of their coreligionists in this country. Rabbi Narot acknowledged that "the sense of responsibility for our fellow Jews the world over, so well known in other areas and until our own time, will continue to make us generous, to sustain that people in every land in which they are to be found." He feels that American Jews should visit Israel, should be impressed by its struggle for economic and political survival and progress. He reported the progress he observed from trip to trip. There are more roads, more autos, more factories, and that sure sign of modern urban growth—pollution. Americans should also give all the emotional, spiritual, and financial support they can. They should be equally zealous to sustain Judaism in the United States, where the future of Judaism is also to be determined.

Of the Russian Jews he further wrote: "Many of the Russian Jewish families have relatives here as they do in Israel. These reunions would be as historic, as precious, and as sentiment laden as they are in Israel. These Russian Jewish emigres would bring to us an aversion to dictatorship which America needs.

"What is more, it would be to Israel's benefit were some of the Russian Jews to settle not only in Israel but elsewhere, notably in the United States. As many Jews the world over believe emphatically, Israel needs a strong and active Jewish life outside Israel, just as the Diaspora needs a strong and vital Israel. In fact, it would be to Israel's benefit, and ours, were the Jews of Russia not compelled to want to live elsewhere. Would that Russia would permit them the freedom to pursue and fulfill their Jewish identity, their Jewish loyalties, and their Jewish aspirations in Russia."

A crisis in his personal life produced a near crisis in the congregation. The members characteristically expected him (as many others do) to be a little more than mortal in some human situations. One congregant reminiscing about her childhood concept of the rabbi said she started out thinking the rabbi was God. Though she outgrew the notion and reached a point where her attitude was hardly reverent, some of the earlier thinking probably survived and was common to a great many others. Consequently, in a congregation where the phenomenon was not at all uncommon, it was quite a shock to discover that the rabbi's marriage to Frieda Brill of Indianapolis, to which two children, David and Ruth, were born, was in trouble. Having followed the course he recommended for his flock in the same circumstances, such as counseling over a long period of time, it became apparent that divorce was the logical solution. The rabbi himself was badly shaken. Certainly he felt that he must resign his post at Temple Israel, possibly that he should resign from the rabbinate altogether. For this once at least he found the Temple board more liberal than he in their thinking. He found the members more aware of his difficulty than he supposed possible, and tolerant enough to accept the idea of divorce. A few members of the congregation found that they could not accept it, and resigned, several of them returning later. His second wife, Helene Rubin Berg, the widow of a physician who had died of cancer, brought three children to the union, Susan, Peter, and Betsy Narot Berg.

In his Rosh Hashanah eve sermon in 1969 at Miami Beach Convention Hall to an assemblage of some four thousand of his members, he urged his listeners to strive for personal betterment through honest self-evaluation. He bared his own life of personal conflict as a case in point. He described the unsuccessful and the successful marriages. He confessed that in his secret depths he had yearned to be a renowned rabbi and had even envied the acclaim others seemed to get. Adon Taft, religious editor, writing in *The Miami Herald*, May 15, 1970, quoted Narot as saying, "There is no end in sight, no (final) goal for me," and concluded that "Joe Narot will never be able to consider himself a success." The rabbi also said at the time, "I want Temple Israel to be not just a synagogue, but a strong religious institution where men, women, and young people find comfort and inspiration, and where they find a challenge for themselves and for the community." Time may mellow him and slow him down but every indication is that he will continue to carry on what he considers to be the good fight.

In his efforts to interpret Reform Judaism to non-Jews in the Miami community, Rabbi Narot is following a precedent firmly established by his predecessors, Kaplan and Zwitman. To their practices he has been able to add a new dimension. Previously there had been exchanging of pulpits, visiting speakers, and on at least one occasion an exchange of congregations between Temple Israel and White Temple Methodist Church. In 1951 this concept was broadened and institutionalized into an annual Institute on Judaism for ministers. All clergymen in the area are invited. The speaker, usually from Hebrew Union College or another similar source, is imported as a visiting authority on some special aspect of the subject for the meeting. In 1962 Maurice Gusman began to underwrite the cost of the program, which had previously been funded by the Temple. Toward the

Institute on Judaism for Ministers, meeting in Gumenick Chapel, 1971

Rabbi Joseph R. Narot [111]

Members of Temple Israel exhibit their artwork, 1960

same cause Rabbi Narot and the Reverend Charles Harris of Holy Trinity Lutheran Church in 1953-54 engaged in a radio series on station WKAT entitled "This We Believe" that ran to some fifty programs.

Temple Israel under Rabbi Narot's leadership remains ready to experiment with new ideas to encourage the congregation's interest and participation. In April 1960 members exhibited their artwork under the management of Al Hurwitz, Art Supervisor for Dade County's public schools. Children of the religious school also showed selected pieces of their work. In February 1969 the rabbi and Cantor Bornstein tried a service set to jazz rhythms. In October of the same year the two presented a multimedia service which they themselves had developed. Sermons are sometimes followed by study in groups, or study directly with the rabbi, for those who choose to remain.

Dr. Narot reviews books extensively, sometimes as sermon topics, more often to special groups like the Temple Sisterhood. He makes the Temple *Bulletin* more than a vehicle for announcements by including letters to the congregation, sermon-ettes, or special topic reports. Friday evening and High Holy Days services are broadcast by radio to the sick, the shut-in, or those at a distance. Like others of his colleagues he would like to do more teaching in educational institutions. He did teach Jewish history for two semesters in 1970-71 at Miami-Dade Junior College, South Campus. The demands of such a schedule of regular appearances make it unfeasible for him to undertake a full course of lecture-discussions. His sermons, lectures, and letters on special occasions and subjects have been collected, published, and widely distributed. The titles indicate the variety of subject matter: *What I Believe About God, Letters to the Now Generation, Why I Am A Jew, For Whom the Rabbi Speaks, A Preface to Well Being, An Introduction to a Faith, A Primer for Temple Life,* and *The Lost Honesty.* Since 1965 his High Holy Days sermons have been distributed in printed book-let form.

Rabbi Narot's disposition to become involved in all aspects of Temple activity, and to some degree in the local and national arena, makes great demands upon his time and energy. Serving a large congregation makes further demands of the same sort. His time must be severely budgeted. His ability to reach large num-bers of people through preaching and writing may also some-times obscure his appeal to individuals. That he cannot see and know all of them is obvious, but a letter in 1966 perhaps ex-pressed the feeling of many others. "It would have been so much worse if you had not let me know that I could come to you with my troubles. Even though I did not come again—just to know I could have was a great help. Beyond that you were kind not to make me feel like an obscure member of a large congregation but rather as if I belonged. . . . "

The rabbi has said that he wishes people who belong to Temple Israel to have an experience rather than merely to be affiliated. He and those around him work energetically and imaginatively to provide an experience that will hold the mem-bers of the congregation to Reform Judaism and to Temple Israel. People must continue to find something to attract them to the synagogue in the central city.

Rabbi Joseph R. Narot [113]

9/Religious Education: The Future of Judaism at Stake

The men and women who founded Temple Israel fifty years ago and directed its course in the first years converged on Miami from diverse directions, places, and backgrounds. Some came from the northeast, principally from New York City. Many were immigrants who very likely had entered the country through New York. Another surprisingly large number came from southern towns and cities, from New Orleans and Atlanta and Richmond and scattered places in between. In the unique case of those Jews from Key West, many moved northward 150 miles to the new land of promise at Miami. Those from New York and from abroad were likely to have Orthodox Jewish educational and family backgrounds. Those from southern sources frequently had only limited association with Jewish communal life, some of them none whatever.

They had one thing in common. They were determined to maintain their cultural and religious identity for themselves and for their children. They particularly feared that in the absence of synagogues and religious schools and the other institutions of Jewish life their sons and daughters might grow up ignorant of their heritage, might drift away in indifference or be assimilated into the vast majority of non-Jews among whom they lived. A good case can be made for the assumption that these people were more anxious about the religious education of their children than about synagogue services for themselves. They saw the future of Judaism in their communities and in the nation at large at stake. As in the Sunday schools and parochial schools of Christians, the religious school is the recruiting ground for the next generation of members. The vitality of a congregation or even of a denomination depends upon constant replenishment of membership.

All these considerations have had some influence upon educational programs at Temple Israel. It is not to be implied that other Jewish congregations are less interested in religious education. Rather, this chapter is the story of one group's efforts to provide this education. Perhaps more is at stake at Temple Israel than in most other congregations. The concept of the synagogue that remains in the central city when most of the congregants reside in the suburbs requires not only that Reform Judaism must be served and preserved, but Temple Israel must remain a principal symbol of it. The religious school lies at the heart of the efforts being made, and it is not limited to the young. One significant generalization about education at Temple Israel is the commitment to provide something for people of all ages. Adult education, although primarily for members of the congregation, is also open to others. There has been a perceptible change in the program for adults from town hall secular-type public forums to an emphasis upon a program of education primarily for members of Temple Israel but with a lecture series open to the general public. A large element of Jewishness is in the content of the program.

The religious school has been and continues to be one of Temple Israel's principal assets. Many parents testify that the opportunity to have their children in the school brought them into the congregation. To many it means traveling relatively long distances when they might be affiliated with a nearby synagogue. Alvin Cassel, for example, recalls that he became a bar mitzvah at Temple Beth David but joined Temple Israel because of the opportunity to continue school. He recalls that Henry D. Williams taught the postconfirmation class very effectively. Cassel continued to study Hebrew through high school and later taught a class discussing the various Jewish communal institutions in the religious school.

The history of the religious school falls largely into two parts. In the first three decades it might be called nonprofessional, as it was dependent upon volunteer services of members of the congregation. Although teachers were usually paid, the stipends were little more than token remuneration. What teachers and administrators lacked in their professional knowledge of subject matter and educational theory and practice, they made up for in sincere zeal for the cause they served. The importance of their work cannot be discounted; they developed the school to a point where it could move into a second phase.

In 1952 when Jacob G. Bornstein came as cantor and educational director, the educational effort was finally institutionalized and made professional. The addition of The Colman A. Zwitman Religious School Building in 1955 recognized the major contribution to religious education made by the rabbi and provided the much needed physical facilities for continuing growth in size and effectiveness. Professionally qualified faculty, paid out of regularly budgeted Temple funds, put the school on a sound fiscal basis. That this could be done without some loss of religious quality is due to the concern of Rabbi Joseph R. Narot, Educational Director Bornstein, and the congregation that everyone associated with the school also should be committed to its underlying purpose of winning students to Judaism and to Temple Israel.

A chronological-topical review of fifty years of effort at the school will illustrate and document the generalizations just stated. When the Jewish community in Miami was small, and before they had a synagogue or a rabbi, there were efforts at religious education. When a visiting rabbi came for High Holy Day services or other special occasions, he might be pressed into giving a few lessons. Any visitor who was suspected of having something to offer was likewise approached. Concerned laymen organized classes and short courses, but with mixed results. This activity mostly reflected the great anxiety of the Jewish residents to have some religious education. Claire Cohen (Mrs. Sydney L.) Weintraub grew up in a pioneer Miami Jewish home, and she recalls that although she had no opportunity to attend a religious school she was asked to teach in one at Temple Beth David. Reba Engler (Mrs. Jack L.) Daner, who came to Miami from Key West in 1912, recalls the discontinuous character of the religious education her parents provided in their determination that she was to have all there was to be had. As a freshman student at Florida State College for Women (now Florida State University) she and a Jacksonville roommate began to teach in the small Jewish community in Tallahassee. They could at least introduce the textbooks and other materials being sent out from Hebrew Union College (HUC) and the Union of American Hebrew Congregations (UAHC) in Cincinnati. When she returned to Miami and married Leonard Epstein, who came from North Carolina, they both taught in the school, and when he died in 1955 he was president of the congregation. Mitchell Wolfson reported that in the Key West community, which contributed so many members to early Temple Israel, Jews there could attend Methodist or Catholic schools. Only those who like himself could be sent away to school would have much opportunity to get a Jewish education.

As the Miami population grew, and with it the Jewish community, professional teachers in the secular schools began to be available to double as religious school teachers. Mrs. I. M. Weinstein came from Nashville, Tennessee, in 1924 to teach English in the Miami High School. She had grown up in Nashville where she was in a Reform congregation and where she earned a degree at the George Peabody College for Teachers. She taught in the religious school, became president of the Sisterhood, and played a prominent role in the congregation. The growing number of Jewish residents and professionally educated teachers in the public schools and the colleges and universities were available educational resources upon which the religious school could draw. The last two superintendents of the religious school before 1952 were Harold Ruby from the public schools and Dr. Donald R. Michelson, Director of Hillel Foundation at the University of Miami and lecturer in history and in humanities, and, since its organization, chairman of the Humanities Division at Miami Dade Junior College, South Campus. Dr. Sidney L. Besvinick, a professor of education and director of the Commission on Academic Goals and Evaluation of Curriculum, and Dr. Ronald B. Newman, an English professor, both at the University of Miami, direct and teach in the adult education series. Such notables as Dr. Mose L. Harvey, specialist in Soviet affairs, and Dr. Sidney W. Fox, director of the Institute of Molecular Evolution, have appeared on the lecture program. Other faculty members from the fields of education, history, philosophy, psychology, and religion have lectured on occasion. Bornstein's professional and career training differed in that it was specifically for teaching and for administration of education and sacred music in a Reform congregation.

Formal, chartered activity at Temple Israel began early in 1923 but had been under way for some time previously. On March 15, 1923, at what was called the eighth meeting of the congregation, three classes were reported, one of them in Hebrew being taught by the newly appointed rabbi, Dr. Salo Stein. Teachers and courses are rarely identified in the records from which this book is taken. When the Sisterhood organized in the fall of 1923, as reported in the succeeding chapter, religious education received its staunchest supporters. Mrs. Morris Plant became the superintendent in November and served until she resigned in 1944 except for five years when she did not reside in Miami. Confusion of the terms principal, superintendent, and chairman in the records makes establishing a clear line of administration difficult. Apparently the chairman of the religious school board sometimes is confused in the record with the principal or superintendent directly responsible for the management of the school. Mrs. Herman I. Homa recalled that she and Rose Davis and Mrs. A. Goldberg were among the early teachers. Although some of the earliest members later stated that they chose a Reform temple because more English and less Hebrew were used in the service, they were not opposed to the teaching of Hebrew. Their attitude reflected rather their total ignorance of the language. In fact, emphasis upon the teaching of Hebrew at Temple Israel has grown steadily. Contributory factors have been the number of boys preparing for the bar mitzvah ceremony, the emergence of the State of Israel with new status for the national language, and the other students who study the language for cultural reasons rather than for any immediate application. Temple Israel, together with Temple Beth David and Temple Beth Jacob, supported David Freedman, the first Hebrew teacher in the Jewish community. He and his wife retired in 1964 after twenty-nine years of teaching, the first sixteen of them at the temples before he joined the Bureau of Jewish Education to teach Hebrew in the high school.

The depression years were hard on the religious school, as on all other phases of life in Greater Miami. The hopeful beginnings in the inflation-minded middle twenties quickly gave way to retrenchment, but never abandonment. In February 1927 teachers who were being paid ten dollars a month were being asked to work without pay. In May of the same year, before he had been the spiritual leader for a full year, Dr. Jacob H. Kaplan in his annual report stated that he was teaching Hebrew and had delivered a number of lectures on Jewish science. He reported a school consisting of nine classes with an average total attendance of near 200 pupils.

In 1928 Rabbi Kaplan's report contained a bit more of his philosophy of religious education. He regretted that the school provided for the needs of children only. Education should not stop at thirteen or sixteen but at the end of life. "The Reform Jew feels that he has a mission and has something to say to the thinking world today. To be able to say this every Jew must be well informed." Again and again he stated his belief that the religious school should be open at least two or three days a week. He felt that teachers should have professional training and be paid accordingly. He looked forward to the time when the Temple could provide means for young men and women to spend the summer at HUC and study at the Teachers' School to learn what was needed in the school and prepare themselves for the work they were offering to do. Mrs. Kaplan was also involved in the religious school and served as superintendent for a time. Dr. Kaplan felt a paid professional choir was necessary to render "the finest Jewish music in an artistic and dependable way." In 1931 he reported that his efforts to maintain a high school were only partially successful, for he had to cancel three classes for lack of teachers. Myron Zeientz exhibits a high school diploma dated May 1930, with Rabbi Kaplan also signing as teacher, and his father, Louis Zeientz, as chairman of the education board. Dorothy (Mrs. Maurice) Serotta, whose high school diploma is dated 1939, recalls that during the war these classes dissolved so completely that afterwards when Rabbi Graff began a high school department many people did not realize that there ever had been one.

Rabbi Kaplan tackled another problem which is almost unique to Miami. Winter residents and visitors were entering and withdrawing their children throughout the school year. In 1930 he recommended that children of unaffiliated visitors be allowed to attend only if they became associate members at fifty dollars a year. In July 1935 the Temple board ruled that pupils of nonmembers or itinerants must pay ten dollars tuition per child or that the family must become associate members at $25.00 a year. Temple Israel now restricts its religious school to children of member families.

By 1936 the worst of the depression years was gone. The membership was beginning to grow, and the demands of the congregation and the community upon the rabbi's time and energy increased. He could not be an all-purpose spiritual leader. He asked for a social secretary to handle all arrangements for social affairs. The board felt that an assistant rabbi who could serve as educational director was more desirable and employed Colman A. Zwitman, who arrived in September. Dr. Kaplan was reluctant to surrender the direction of the religious school, but Zwitman was an admirable choice, and the senior rabbi gave him a relatively free hand and continued to teach some courses, particularly to prepare youth for confirmation.

Dorothy Serotta recalled thirty years later that the confirmation classes did not appreciate nearly enough his wide knowledge of philosophy and history.

In 1929 Rabbi Kaplan had been authorized to employ the necessary number of teachers for the religious school to be paid $50.00 each for the school year. At the same time the Sisterhood denied his request for a printing press to turn out a paper for Sunday school children and for Temple notices. In May 1939 Mrs. Plant reported to the congregation that 200 were enrolled in a dozen classes, twelve of the students studying Hebrew. Rabbi Kaplan was instructing a confirmation class of twenty-five. Significantly, $1,100 annually was being provided for the support of the school. In 1942 the ladies agreed to pay a salary to the "principal." The next year the Temple board agreed to share all school costs with the Sisterhood, each providing $1,000. Ten teachers would receive three dollars each Sunday, and the librarian, the secretary, and the Hebrew teacher would each receive five dollars. In 1944 the two sponsors each provided $1,500. The next year the board assumed all financial responsibility for the religious school.

The Sisterhood had not abandoned education but would devote its funds to youth programs for students beyond the school age. In 1949, for example, they voted to defray half the expense of sending young people to a youth conclave of Reform Judaism in Albany, Georgia. The following year they agreed that the receipts of the Constance Pearlman Fund, established a year earlier to be administered in the best interests of the religious school, should be used to provide professional leadership of youth groups. In 1951 they sent students to Sky Lake Camp in Sautee, Georgia, and the next year they helped send six students to the same camp. In 1956 a youth camp counselor for the National Federation of Temple Youth (NFTY) received $300, and funds were voted to send Temple Israel delegates to the Southeastern Federation of Temple Youth (SEFTY) camps.

Increasing efforts to provide training for teachers are also a part of the story. In March 1939 Rabbi Zwitman announced to the board that teachers would receive a course of lectures by the outstanding Jewish educator, Dr. Emanuel Gamoran, chairman of the Commission on Education for the UAHC. Classes would be organized as round table forums of a specific classroom nature. Teachers of other religious schools would also participate, and the several Sisterhoods would pay the expenses. In May Rabbi Zwitman attended the annual meeting of the Central Conference of American Rabbis as a member of the committee on Jewish Education. While in New York he proposed to study Christian Sunday schools. During his vacation in 1938 he had reported he would make a study of the larger New York Jewish schools and examine the textbooks they were using. Upon his return he and Mrs. Plant would make final decisions and submit orders for school materials. On March 1, 1948, Max Meisel, chairman of the Bureau of Jewish Education, sponsored an eight week seminar for Sunday school and day school teachers and an evening course in Hebrew.

A serious handicap to the school and an absolute limit in size was lack of space. Classes met in small rooms in Kaplan Hall, actually the lower floor of the sanctuary, with only temporary dividers which did not insulate the classes against the noise from adjoining groups. In March 1941 Mrs. Plant urged that heaters be placed in the rooms. The Sisterhood came to the rescue and purchased heaters in February 1942. On January 10, 1950, Mrs. Morris Wolff at the first Sisterhood meeting after Rabbi Zwitman's death stated the reasons for a new religious school building. She proposed that they ask President Max Orovitz to take the matter to the Temple board and the congregation. Out of this proposal grew The Colman Zwitman Religious School Building in 1955.

The coming of Education Director Bornstein moved the religious school into the modern phase. The employment of a full-time professional responsible for education and music was a long, double step. Some members had doubts about the inclusion of a cantor, but the response was generally enthusiastic as time passed. Dorothy Serotta recalls, "Then came Cantor Bornstein and religious school began to belong to my children instead of me ... from the beginning his music and his idealism and his pleasant simpleness have made the profoundest impression on all of them, as well as on me. The new building, the new music, the new bar mitzvah ceremonies (we had almost none before the war), the new spirit of the school were all his doing. .... " Making the transition to professional teachers was not easy for the administrators of the school. Not that they were depriving former teachers of a livelihood—the pay for the once-a-week services was nominal. Harold Thurman, chairman of the education board, described as horrifying and almost personally devastating the experience of telling women who had taught for twenty or even thirty years that their services were no longer required; "but we were putting the children ahead of the people."

The changes since 1952 are not to be measured in the numbers of classes, teachers, and students. School enrollment has not grown as rapidly as has membership in the congregation. Superintendent Michelson reported 325 pupils in 1952. Twenty years later the director reported over 800 registered students, some fifty faculty members, and an annual budget of close to $50,000. A cost accounting fixed the per pupil cost for 1971-72 at $138. Perhaps it is not too much to say that new approaches have kept the school alive. The most important result is a school in which pupils have more than a passive interest, that indifference if not outright opposition has been converted into positive interest and achievement.

The basic change has been from a conventional school approach in which traditional courses have long been considered a necessary part of the preparation of boys and girls for confirmation to a curriculum and, more exactly, an approach that is built upon student interest and motivation. The program also has been extended to all age groups. As in more progressive contemporary secular education, the most important objective is to make the offering meaningful and relevant rather than to have new courses. The keynote is the exploratory and experimental character of the approach.

In 1952 Jacob G. Bornstein completed a course in education

and sacred music at Hebrew Union College. His was the second class to graduate. The two parts of the course were not unrelated; both required intimate knowledge of the Hebrew language and Jewish culture which could be translated into music and education. Obviously the combination of natural vocal endowment and interest and administrative ability in the running of a religious school are rarely to be found in one person. That they are ideally associated in the case of Jack Bornstein has been demonstrated at Temple Israel.

One early change was to increase the time given to the study of Hebrew by having classes meet during the week. The administration recognized that if the language was to be useful and meaningful it must be mastered to a degree impossible in classes that met only one day a week. This is a problem with which secular schools are wrestling. For the baccalaureate degree too much or too little language is required. Too much time is spent on it for the benefits derived unless enough more time is spent to make it a usable knowledge. The result from the changes at Temple Israel has been an increase in the number of people studying Hebrew. From an enrollment of thirteen in 1953, Hebrew classes have grown to 170 pupils taught in three locations to make travel easier: one in North Miami, one in Coral Gables (at West Laboratory School), and the third at the Temple.

Faculty for the religious school is carefully chosen. In addition to their knowledge of subject matter, the faculty must have some kind of Jewish background, if not formal Jewish education, and they must have demonstrated interest in working at child development. In-service training is provided in seminars, in frequent meetings with the director and the rabbinical staff, and on weekend retreats at which objectives and ways and means to achieve them are discussed. Radical changes in the preparation for confirmation now encourage the students to look beyond confirmation by involving them in the educational program in ways that will induce them to continue into the high school program and remain closely associated with Temple Israel.

The Religious School Board has frequently gone outside the community to have the educational program evaluated. In November 1957 the board invited Libbie (Mrs. Sigmund) Braverman, for more than twenty years educational director of the Euclid Avenue Temple in Cleveland, Ohio, to make a survey. She had studied the curriculum and other records of the school before she arrived in Miami. She began her visit by speaking from the pulpit on Friday evening. On Saturday and on Sunday morning she visited the school in session. In a luncheon and afternoon session on Sunday she met with teachers and administrators, and on Monday she reported to the school board at another luncheon. In addition to a detailed report on specific items she pronounced the school superior in all respects except parent participation. The adult program now provided on Sundays is designed in part to provide something for parents while children are in their classes.

The changes grew out of a survey of pupil interest at Temple Israel made by Morris Janowitz, chairman of the Department of Sociology at the University of Chicago, with the assistance of Roberta Ash, of the University of Chicago Center for Social Organization Studies, and published in 1969 under the title *Judaism of the Next Generation.* It has had a large sale in Jewish, Protestant, and Catholic religious schools. In March 1957 a student council made up of representatives from fifth grade and up began to help make known the views of religious school students, but the student council lacked the depth and authority sought in the new study. The study involved 268 boys and girls, mainly in the 12 to 15 age group, attending religious school in 1966. From this somewhat sophisticated and certainly professional study, some conclusions significant to an educational program emerge. The youngsters emphasized a religious rather than an ethnic or cultural self-conception of their Jewishness. At the same time a concern with relevant personal and social ethics is a central part of their religious interest, and they are searching for a cultural basis for their Jewish identity beyond that which comes from religious doctrine. The fact that Judaic thought is subject to continuous redefinition is a positive attraction for a group of students taught in secular school to be self-critical. They are caught up in the dilemma that they wish to maintain their Jewish affiliation and equally to insist on having patterns of intimate friendship with non-Jews. Very importantly, the students exhibit an overriding concern with personal relevance in their attitude toward Temple education. The pressure of contemporary concerns is too great to make the study of the Bible and Talmud, or the history and philosophy of Judaism, their favorite subjects. Interest in comparative religion is part of a desire to give direct and immediate meaning to Judaism by contemporary rather than historical study. They seek cultural content and symbols which fit into the American scene and at the same time give contemporary meaning to Jewish social cohesion. They are likely to study Hebrew not because it relates to the study of history but because it is a visible and acceptable sign of being a Jew.

The course of study at Temple Israel was redesigned to draw upon the interests and attitudes discovered, and these were not considered final, for it was recognized that interests and attitudes will continue to change. In the elementary school, grades from kindergarten through six, a theme is selected for each Sunday, to be studied at all levels at the same time. In preparation, faculty meet with the director and the rabbinic staff to explore ways and means to present the unit of study. From their homerooms children go to a workshop of their choice but one related to the central theme of the day.

For the junior high school group of seventh, eighth, and ninth grades, the largely neglected middle school group, often overlooked in studies of educational theory and practice, the adjustment is different. Instead of weekly meetings on Saturday or Sunday morning, an experience beginning on Friday evening and running all day Saturday is offered once a month. It is run like a conference, with a central theme and the presentation of basic materials. The students then break up into workshop and discussion groups. When questions were raised about the shofar, Dr. Leslie Bukstel demonstrated how to make and sound one and in the process presented the whole story of its significance in the ritual. Though it is early to judge, the result appears good. The quality of the learning experience is improved, and an in-

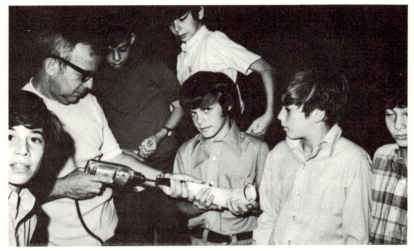

Teacher Dr. Leslie T. Bukstel and students fashion a shofar.

creasing number of students continue in the high school program. Traditionalists wonder if allowing such a wide choice of learning activity is religious. Proponents point out that any activity can be religious, that it is useful to pursue any idea at all, that the boys and girls also discover their talents and involve many adults in the congregation.

Nowhere in the Temple Israel program is the accent on youth more obvious than in the high school age group. The religious school for this group began in 1958 when Assistant Rabbi Graff reestablished it. He began with only six students. The principal instruction was provided by Rabbi Graff and Rabbi Narot. The program now serves about 200 students. The greatest present emphasis is upon youth activities, the most important of which are retreats combining recreation and music with serious discussion. The Sisterhood has strongly supported these retreats, making them their most important educational concern. Young assistant rabbis have been brought in to work with younger people: Steve Jacobs, Barry Tabachnikoff, and Nicolas Behrmann. A nearby place for retreats that will reduce travel time and make frequent trips more possible has now been acquired.

Religious Education [127]

Adult education is not new, but the focus is. Until recently it consisted of programs of general interest directed at the general public. The subjects and spokesmen were only incidentally, if at all, Jewish. In the very first year of the Temple's existence Dr. Salo Stein, the rabbi, wrote to inquire if Rabbi Stephen S. Wise was coming to Miami the following winter and if the new congregation might present him to the community and hear him. In 1940-41, the Men's Clubs of the Temple and the White Temple Methodist Church were presenting the Town Hall Forum. In 1962 Myron and Evelyn Behrmann made sponsorship of the secular forum a Temple Israel affair. In 1965 they brought in Norman Cousins, Henry A. Kissinger, John Kenneth Galbraith, and Philip Burton. After four years this program was superseded by the Eugene and Shirley Greenfield Institute for Adult Studies. The program is primarily, although not exclusively, for members of the congregation. For 1971-72 it included ten visiting lecturers with programs directed at a wider audience. It also

Temple Israel presented the Ginsberg poets, father and son, on December 21, 1969. Left to right: Rabbi Narot, Rabbi Steven B. Jacobs, Allen Ginsberg, Louis Ginsberg, and Edward Cohen.

provided twenty-two weeks of classes beginning September 12 under the direction of University of Miami Professors Sidney L. Besvinick and Ronald Newman. The basic registration and attendance for these sessions consists primarily of the families with children in Sunday school at the same time. The theme of the series was "The Jew: Self and Society." A sampling of the lecture topics by visitors who appeared between November 21 and March 19 will provide an indication of the range of topics and interests. On December 5 Philosopher Abraham Kaplan of the University of Michigan discussed "The Psychology of Women and the Meaning of Love"; on February 13 Rabbi Robert Gordis of the Jewish Theological Seminary spoke on "The Social, Political and Economic Ideals of the Bible"; on February 20 Dr. Karl Menninger presented a seminar on "The Crime of Punishment: A Look at Prison Reform"; on March 5 Sister Margaret Traxler, acting director of the National Catholic Conference for Interracial Justice, discussed "The Roman Catholic Church in Ferment;" and on March 19 Miss Sally Priesand, the first woman rabbi, ordained in June 1972 at Hebrew Union College, explained "A Woman Rabbi: Her Problems, Prerogatives and Principles."

In 1968-69 the Greenfield Institute for Adult Studies had as its theme "Sociological Factors in American Judaism." Perhaps it was partly reaction to that institute which induced Rabbi Narot to query in December of 1969, "Should we employ a full-time psychiatric caseworker?" He said that he and Assistant Rabbi Jacobs could easily spend all their time on the problems of marijuana and drugs and on psychological and parental problems in the religious school. William and Irene Siegel provided funds for employing a psychiatric caseworker for a year of trial. The Temple board funded the program for several short extensions thereafter but finally terminated it for lack of funds.

Continuing interest in the community outside the congregation and concern about the problems of society, particularly in the area of the central city where the synagogue is located, were demonstrated graphically in 1964-65 in an experimental kindergarten for deprived children, aptly called by a newswriter "A

Pre-Head Start class taught by Mrs. Joan Bornstein under the auspices of Temple Israel.

School for Catching Up." The school grew out of the work of the Temple's social action committee. In cooperation with the Dade County Public Schools and the Florida Department of Public Welfare, they explored the possibility that youngsters can overcome the handicap of a limited environment. For the project thirteen five-year olds were selected from the central Negro district. Only six of them had both parents, and only two had telephones at home. Some of them could hardly speak, and little socialization of their conduct had been developed. The children could not be assumed to know even simple things. Free dental and medical services were available. A psychiatrist examined each child, and a welfare social worker visited each home. The project was directed by Joan (Mrs. Jacob) Bornstein, who had been trained in early childhood education and had taught deprived children in New York City. The results were dramatic. How lasting the effects on the children may be is questionable. The effect of the program on the Temple staff and members who watched the personalities of the children emerge and develop is everlasting. They know by experience and observation what the Head Start programs instituted since that time under public auspices can achieve. Some of these Head Start classes, incidentally, meet in Temple Israel classrooms. As we worked in the Temple library during the pre-Christmas season, the sound of children singing Christmas carols was frequently heard.

The experimental project raised again the question of the congregation's obligation to the community. How far should Temple Israel members go to provide services, particularly in the fields of education, health, and welfare, which society now increasingly provides through all levels of government for all citizens? The same question arises about the maintenance of hospitals and educational institutions designated as Jewish but open equally to non-Jews. Max Orovitz points out that not many years ago there were very tangible reasons. Jewish medical students, interns, and doctors needed a place to study and practice. For these reasons he supported the development of Mount Sinai Hospital, and also the nonsectarian University of Miami Medical School, which promised no quota system and no discrimination. The University of Miami recently made another Temple member, Dr. Milton M. Coplan, an honorary alumnus for his work in starting the University's Medical School twenty years ago. The kind of exclusion practices Orovitz was fighting has largely disappeared, but the communal sense of responsibility continues to induce Jews to support such medical institutions, as well as institutions for the aged. Gerald Lewis and A. J. Harris from Temple Israel have also served on the Mount Sinai Board of Directors of which Orovitz was for some years the chairman. Abe Aronovitz was much interested in the building of the nonsectarian Cedars of Lebanon Hospital, and his contribution is recognized in the Abe Aronovitz Memorial Pavilion. Other Temple Israel members on that hospital's board were Elliott Blumenthal, Joseph Garfield, Harry Lewis, Sam Luby, Sr., and David Stuzin.

The effort to identify as much activity as possible with Temple Israel has not meant that the institution or its members reject responsible roles in common enterprises of the Jewish community. The best example is the Greater Miami Jewish Federation organized in 1938 after a meeting in the home of Sam Blank to coordinate planning and fund raising for programs of common interest. In 1939 Baron de Hirsch Meyer headed the first Combined Jewish Appeal. Other Temple members who have since headed the federation are Max Orovitz, William D. Singer, Aaron Kanner, Benjamin Bronston, Monte Selig, Dan B. Ruskin, Howard Kane, and Robert Russell, currently vice-president of Temple Israel and the federation president.

H. Franklin Williams presents National Conference of Christians and Jews citation to Max Orovitz, 1943. Harold Turk, seated.

10/"This Faithful Band of Workers in Israel": The Sisterhood

Women helped to organize Temple Israel. They have given it loving devotion and tangible sustenance since the beginning. The practice of listing families rather than individuals in the membership rolls sometimes obscures their identity, but their place in this history is made secure by the most complete records in the Temple archives. When Sie Mendelson arrived in Miami in 1921, he found Mrs. Harry Simons and Mrs. Morris Gusky actively recruiting members for the new congregation. Mrs. Mendelson and Mrs. Nat Roth were among those who attended meetings in homes before a formal organization could be made. Eight women signed the charter application approved by Judge F. H. Atkinson on May 31, 1923. They were Mrs. A. J. Applebaum, Mrs. M. L. Cowen, Mrs. Frank Elfman, Mrs. Gusky, Mrs. M. C. Hodes, Mrs. Max Nankin, Mrs. Morris Plant, and Mrs. Roth.

The Temple Israel Sisterhood met for formal organization on September 18, 1923, in the Young Men's Hebrew Association (YMHA) rooms in the Seybold Building on Flagler Street. Rabbi Louis Egelson, assistant director of the synagogue and school extension department at Hebrew Union College (HUC) in Cincinnati had come down to preach the High Holy Days sermons. He met with the ladies, consulted with them about effecting their organization, and promised to send a model constitution. In attendance were Mrs. W. Apte, Mrs. Gusky, Mrs. Hodes, Mrs. Herman I. Homa, Mrs. Mendelson, Mrs. A. Molnar, Mrs. C. Peyser, Mrs. Roth, Mrs. Max Springer, and Mrs. Louis Zeientz. As temporary officers Mrs. Springer became chairman and Mrs. Zeientz became secretary. Mrs. Roth headed a membership committee, and Mrs. Homa's group was responsible for the constitution and bylaws.

At the second meeting an entertainment committee began to function. This usually meant fund raising. The first card party on October 22 earned thirty-three dollars, and card parties continued in an endless chain for months and years, usually in the homes of members. This group consisted largely of younger women, and Sisterhood activities provided almost all their social life. Mrs. Mendelson recalled nearly fifty years later: "It was something new and we were just looking for something to do." Her husband recalls, "We didn't have concerts and plays. There was only 40,000 population. In the summertime you could shoot a cannon down Flagler Street and there was nothing to hit."

Before they had completed the procedures for organization, the ladies were taking the lead in the establishment of a religious school on November 4, 1923. Mrs. Harriett Bulbin, a recent president of Sisterhood, feels that mothers have always been more conscious of the importance of religious education and more ready to accept responsibility for it. They are more likely to have the task of bringing up the children. Mrs. Morris Plant became the superintendent, and Mrs. Homa and Mrs. A. Goldberg (Granger), Sisterhood members, were among the first teachers. Nonmembers and visitors were invited to send their children. There were no fees and no pay for teachers. The role of the women's auxiliary in the educational program has been described to some extent in the preceding chapter.

On November 5, 1923, the organization chose its permanent officers. Mrs. Plant became president; Mrs. Springer, first vice-president; Mrs. Molnar, second vice-president; Mrs. Mendelson, recording secretary; Mrs. J. Katz, corresponding secretary; Mrs. A. B. Cromer, financial secretary; Mrs. Zeientz, treasurer; and three directors were Mrs. Cowen, Mrs. Gusky, and Mrs. Louis Wolfson.

The Temple's treasury was the principal beneficiary of the Sisterhood's money-raising efforts. By Febrary 1924 they had collected $801.30. Activities included a Jolly Measuring Party with prizes for the smallest and largest girth. Mrs. Homa, an early president of the group, recently recalled, "We had bazaars. The women worked like Trojans. Nothing was too much for them to do. We had suppers. We had everything that you could think of that would make money. We had cake sales. We baked cookies. I can't think of anything we didn't do." In April 1924 the women's organization provided and prepared the food and supplied Haggadoth for a Passover seder. The project netted $107.83 and became a regular feature of Temple life.

The interest of the enterprising women extended beyond the welfare of their own congregation. Rabbi Joseph Jasin spoke on current events at one meeting. The women protested lack of Jewish representation in the Community Chest and began to participate in that effort. They helped to raise money for Hebrew Aid of Miami. When the rabbi spoke of the terrible conditions existing among immigrant Jews in Cuba and the lack of concern in that country, the Sisterhood sent him to Havana to investigate. He reported that the problems were too serious for the Temple to tackle and sent his report to others who might be better able to do something about them.

The Temple Israel group immediately joined the National Federation of Temple Sisterhoods (NFTS) and thereafter sold Uniongrams, a complete card service for all occasions, to support its work. In May 1926 they voted to join the Dade County Federation of Women's Clubs. They supported the organization of a chapter of Hadassah. They provided flowers for the pulpit at all services and cared for the Temple and its properties, usually performing the labor themselves. A sewing committee made altar scarves and lined the Ark. The same leadership made arrangements for music, paying $35.00 a month in 1924 to Mrs.

Iva Sproul Baker, an organist, while they themselves made up the choir, and one of them, Gertrude Cowen, sang solos. When the time came to abandon the temporary synagogue on Northeast Fourteenth Street in the summer of 1926, they packed the movable property for transfer.

By the summer of 1925 the Sisterhood counted seventy-three dues-paying members. In January 1926, in a new venture, they sponsored a concert at White Temple Methodist Church featuring Maria Winetzkia, a noted vocalist. The widely publicized and well-attended event left them a profit of $954.89. Accumulated funds were used to turn over to the Temple treasury $500, to purchase kindergarten furniture and 200 prayer books, and to pay Sunday school teachers ten dollars a month.

In reality the ladies were beginning to be caught up in the inflationary spirit engendered by the spiraling real estate boom.

Pioneer Sisterhood members at the donor luncheon, April 1972. Seated left to right: Mrs. Mitchell Kuperberg, Mrs. H. I. Homa, Mrs. Sie Mendelson, Mrs. Harry Hirsch, and Mrs. Harry Nevins. Standing left to right: Mrs. Isaac Wolkowsky, Mrs. Hazel Dallett, Mrs. Sylvia Sprintz, Mrs. Frances Abrams, and Mrs. Isaac Levin.

Those who were not yet being enriched by it had the feeling that they inevitably would be. This notion was reflected by the liberal manner in which they supported activities far afield. They made what were for them substantial contributions to the Denver Home for Tubercular Children, The Jewish National Hospital in Denver, and the Hebrew Union College Dormitory Fund. Mrs. Mendelson recalls laughingly how they were being free with their hard-earned money little knowing how soon they themselves might have dire need of it. When hard times came, as they soon did, the women spent no time on regrets but worked the harder for the survival of Temple Israel.

Mrs. Herman Homa headed the Sisterhood from 1926 to 1928, during which time membership reached 129. When Rabbi Jacob H. Kaplan came to Temple Israel in 1926, he had served in several congregations and knew the worth of the ladies' auxiliary. In his first annual report in 1927 he listed all their accomplishments for the year and gave them the characterization that heads this chapter. They had paid for a copy of *Young Israel* for every child in the upper classes of the religious school, had provided entertainment and refreshments for several holidays, had served congregational dinners—one of them in cooperation with the Men's Club—and had furnished flowers for Temple occasions; the flowers were later distributed to the sick and shut-in. A dinner dance they sponsored at the Coral Gables Country Club Kaplan pronounced perfect in every detail. They had provided singers for the choir and conducted services in the Temple on Women's Day, also called Sisterhood Sabbath, which included preaching the sermon. The women had obligated themselves to purchase an organ for the new sanctuary, then under construction. Their delegates had attended the national meeting in Cleveland and the regional sessions in Atlanta.

Before the new structure was completed and dedicated in 1928, Miamians were beginning to feel the effects of the deepening Florida depression which followed the collapse of the land boom and the 1926 hurricane. Members of the Sisterhood worked more seriously at fund raising and spent their money more grudgingly. National causes received five or ten dollars whereas in the more flush days twenty-five or fifty dollars was not uncommon. The Sisterhood was meeting temporarily in the Women's Club Building, the Central School Building, and the Seventh Day Adventist Church until their own sanctuary could be completed. Membership fell to 108 in the spring of 1928. They played host to the State Federation of Sisterhoods that year. They raised $2,527.83 by their activities, one of which was a garden party that remained an annual feature on their schedule. Braille transcription, which later became a major activity, is first discussed as a project in the minutes of that year. Congresswoman Ruth Bryan Owen addressed a meeting on "The Organization of Relief Work in the State." War and peace was the topic for discussion at another meeting, and an annual meeting devoted to a discussion of peace became a regular feature of their program.

Temple Israel, like almost every other institution and individual in the country, entered the Florida depression overcommitted, and the national depression starting late in 1929 hit them before there were any real signs of recovery. The commitment to purchase the organ proved a burden for some years. The instrument did long service and, when it was replaced, was donated to Mt. Zion Baptist Church. The ladies found themselves also asked to pick up the commitment for kitchen equipment, and this has been a continuing project. Austerity became the order of the day. Some of the fun had gone out of Sisterhood activities, but not the pledge to do whatever was necessary to keep Temple services going. The women rejected the suggestion that they cease giving the reception after the service on Friday nights. They did make one concession to the depression; they would buy flowers at the curb market instead of from the florist which meant a 75 percent saving, from two dollars a bunch to fifty cents.

In 1931 Rabbi Kaplan began teaching a Bible study class for Sisterhood members. He also served as adviser to a child study class directed by Mrs. J. Gerald Lewis. Mrs. Kaplan helped to organize a program of youth activities. Another appeal to the interest of youth was a reception and dance in December to which alumni of the Temple religious school and all junior University of Miami students were invited. A Sisterhood luncheon that year was billed as a get-together "to promote good fellowship among the Jewish women of the City."

The Sisterhood continued its strong support of the religious school. They resisted the proposal that teachers work without pay and, except for a brief period, raised the money for at least token payments. During Mrs. I. M. Weinstein's presidency (1933-34), a thousand dollars was budgeted for teachers' pay. The women tackled a formidable problem in the sanctuary. The seats were covered with a plastic that became sticky in warm weather. During a service a crackling sound occurred as women's dresses were peeled off the seats when they stood for prayers. When President Isaac Levin of the congregation and Mrs. Weinstein asked for bids to re-cover the seating, the cost proved prohibitive. They elected as a temporary expedient to cover the seats with cotton toweling, the women doing the work. "It wasn't gorgeous; it wasn't beautiful; it was strictly functional," and they used it for several years.

In 1935 when the Temple negotiated an $18,000 loan to refinance the outstanding indebtedness on the sanctuary, the Sisterhood gave the obligation a high priority until it was paid off ten years later. This did not mean neglect of any of the usual expenditures. In fact, they made at least one contribution of $250 toward the payment of arrears in the rabbi's salary.

The late thirties and early forties were a period of transition in the community and in the Temple. The worst of the depression was past. Business was improving. The Jewish community began to grow rapidly as did membership in the congregation. The first generation of leadership in the Temple and in auxiliary organizations, after two decades of effort, began to be less active. The relatively small, close-knit group struggling against economic odds was giving way to larger numbers. Many of the newcomers were unacquainted with the struggle for survival that had gone on for so long. For a time meetings were held irregularly while adjustments to new conditions were being worked out in a somewhat groping fashion. Temple Israel was also beginning to feel for the first time the effects of suburban growth. Whereas in the early days the members had lived largely in the Miramar section of Miami, where the Temple is now located, this was no longer true. One solution, reportedly successful in other places, tried and abandoned at Temple Israel, was to hold regional meetings throughout Greater Miami where members resided in sufficient numbers. It was highly important for the future of Temple Israel that the members preferred to have Sisterhood activities continue to be associated with the synagogue on Northeast Nineteenth Street.

Also, the highly personal character of much Sisterhood activity was about to become more institutionalized. The larger membership and the improved economic outlook made possible increased budgets of support for Temple activities. Small and informal events began to be replaced by a series of regularly scheduled annual affairs in which the members were less directly involved.

The Second World War was a matter of grave concern to the Jewish community. Added to their concern as citizens of the United States was their anxiety over the fate of Jews in Europe and especially in Palestine. After Hitler's invasion of Poland in 1939, war clouds gathered quickly, and the effects became apparent in the United States long before December 1941 when the bombings at Pearl Harbor precipitated our entry into the conflict. Late in 1940 the Temple Israel Sisterhood formed a Red Cross Committee headed by Mrs. Samuel Katz, Mrs. Harry Boyell, and Mrs. J. E. Freehling. This group began by meeting once a week to sew and knit for hospitals and soldiers. Mounting concern in the congregation was reflected in the minutes of board meetings, the Temple *Bulletin,* and the statements of Rabbis Kaplan and Zwitman. At the meeting in October 1941, Dr. Kaplan, then rabbi emeritus, greeted the ladies and urged them to apply Israel's undaunted spirit of beginning anew in spite of dark days. Though there is no specific reference in the record to the entry of the United States into the war, all groups in the Temple accelerated their efforts in support of war-related activities. Mrs. Isaac Levin, defense chairman of the Sisterhood,

A Passover seder provided by the Sisterhood for servicemen in 1943. In the foreground right to left: Adolph Wertheimer, who planned so many dinners at the Temple; Frank Coret, president of the congregation; Rabbi Zwitman; and Mrs. Zwitman.

explained the function of the Dade County Civilian Defense Agency to make the community self-sufficient in case of an emergency. Members were urged to enroll in nutrition and gardening classes, to purchase defense stamps and bonds, and to send a telegram to Mrs. Franklin D. Roosevelt pledging support for the Civilian Defense Program. Mrs. Harold Spaet directed a first aid course. The Temple kitchen became a unit in the Dade County nutrition plans.

An immediate concern was the welfare of servicemen in the area. The ladies supported the USO canteen on Biscayne Boulevard. Members were asked to invite servicemen and women to their homes. Armed forces personnel were invited to Purim and Passover observances at which Sisterhood members served as hostesses and prepared the food, no easy matter when many items were scarce and rationed. When the conflict was drawing to a close, Mrs. Saul Applebaum, wife of the wartime rabbi, accepted the chairmanship of a victory bond drive and in December 1945 reported $101,825 in bond sales.

The wartime activity restored something of the close-knit associations of earlier days. Because of restriction on travel, the rationing of food, and blackouts, keeping Temple activities going was not easy. The Sisterhood continued the reception following the Friday evening service, but suspended all other social events not directly related to the religious school. Service to the Jewish blind, started shortly before the war, also continued.

In 1945 life was returning to normal even before the conflict was formally terminated. Trends apparent before the rude interruption became obvious again. The Temple board assumed financial responsibility for the religious school, and the Sisterhood concentrated on youth activities. On March 4, 1946, the president, Reba (Mrs. Leonard) Epstein welcomed 200 of the 412 members to a meeting. In 1947, Mrs. Isaac Levin became president for a third, nonconsecutive period. Past presidents have usually remained active in Sisterhood after their term expired, but Mrs. Levin is unique in that she served as president from 1931 to 1933, again from 1935 to 1937, and yet again from 1947 to 1949.

A new venture in 1948 was probably inspired by Rabbi Colman Zwitman, who served on the Family Service Board. The Sisterhood became one of the sponsors of a family service radio series on station WIOD entitled "Marriage for the Millions." In 1949, after the death of an especially loved member associated with the group, the women established the Constance Z. Pearlman Memorial Fund with which they purchased a spinet piano for the religious school building that was being proposed and other religious school needs.

When Rabbi Zwitman died in December 1949, the Sisterhood members agreed that a new building for the religious school was the most fitting memorial to a rabbi who had a way with children and had done so much for the school. Sisterhood minutes report a pledge in 1955 to raise $10,000 a year for five years. Raising the sum brought out some of the inventiveness that always could be tapped when new sources of money were needed. Rummage sales, bazaars, and donor luncheons on a grander scale became part of the effort.

In 1951 the Sisterhood opened a gift shop later named the Judaica Shop that grew into a continuing source of income. Ruby Fogel (Mrs. Jack Levkoff) contributes to the Sisterhood the royalties on all her books of poetry sold in their shop. Her best known book is *Of Ships and Angels.* Her books have won recognition at the Strand Festival of Arts in England and the James Joyce Award of the Poetry Society of America. Members of the Sisterhood had a large share in selling advertising and preparing the Dedication Book for the new education building in 1955. The program included a summary of Sisterhood activity to that time.

Temple and Sisterhood membership grew steadily in the 1950s. By 1957 the size of the Temple board, which is determined by the number of members, had risen from an original ten to fifty. Sisterhood membership reached six hundred. Although many social functions continued to be held at the Temple, an increasing number were catered by professionals rather than prepared and served by members, and others were held at new hotels on Miami Beach.

As Temple Israel grew to be the largest Reform congregation in the Southeast, the role of its auxiliary groups in regional and national organizations began to grow. Temple Israel sent delegates to annual meetings, and its members served on national boards and committees. In 1943 Mrs. Morris Plant began a six-year term on the national Sisterhood board. Others since that time, all presidents of the local group, were Mrs. Leopold Schwartz, Mrs. Aaron Kanner, and Mrs. Joseph Bulbin. In 1963 Mrs. Kanner was also president of the southeastern regional federation which includes Alabama, Florida, Georgia, and South Carolina. Several times the local Sisterhood has received awards for participation in the Youth Educational and Sisterhood (YES) Fund through the sale of Uniongrams for the support of eight national youth camps, the education of rabbinical students, and for educational and instructional materials for the Sisterhood.

Their strong interest in youth activity was demonstrated again in 1952 when at their invitation, Mrs. Julia Hennig, a representative of the NFTS, came to Miami to conduct workshops on interfaith and youth educational projects. In the immediate postwar years there was great concern to improve intergroup and international relations. The National Conference of Christians and Jews received more support. The Sisterhood began an annual interfaith meeting to coincide with Brotherhood week. The concerned ladies also organized a dance cotillion to promote social interaction among Temple youth. They were also one of the sponsors of the local chapter of the National Federation of Temple Youth (NFTY) and paid for a professional counselor's part-time services. They also gave early support to the increasingly popular retreats by providing means for local youth to attend the national and regional camp conclaves. In 1956 a camp fund became the regular means of achieving that goal.

In postwar years the Temple Israel Sisterhood contributed to the fund for the House of Living Judaism which has helped to build the headquarters of the Union of American Hebrew Congregations in New York. Through the Sisterhood Development Fund, the NFTS pledged a million dollars to be raised by Temple chapters to enlarge the House of Living Judaism and provide a new dormitory at HUC and new camps for children. The local chapter accepted $6,000 as its share. By annual contributions and by encouraging private donations, the local group also participates in the World Union of Progressive Judaism which provides for the education and ordination of rabbis of foreign countries, largely by private donations. Similar financial support through NFTS has contributed to the extension of HUC campuses in Los Angeles, Cincinnati, New York, and Jerusalem. A more recent project, supported by voluntary individual donations, is the synagogue at the Ben Shemen Children's Village in Lod, Israel. This village serves as a workshop for Reform Judaism where children have a place for assembly and education. It is also part of an organized effort to introduce Reform into Israel, which is officially Orthodox.

The Sisterhood sewing committee that had been so busy during the war has continued its activity ever since. The members began by providing clothing for children at Dade County's Youth Hall. Recently they have made garments for patients aboard the hospital ship sponsored by Project Hope. Through the same project the sewing committee supplies blankets and other items for American Indians in New Mexico.

Another long-established activity is service to the Jewish blind. The Braille workshop trains Sisterhood members to transcribe books into Braille. Before a member can begin to translate into Braille, she must be certified by the Library of Congress. A Braille manuscript must be prepared and submitted as a basis for certification. Temple Israel has fourteen certified Braillists, several of whom are qualified to do Braille music. Braillists usually have their own machines. The Sisterhood supplies paper, has a blind person proofread it, and pays for binding. They usually braille for the Jewish Braille Institute of America, but they have been known to do it for the blind of other faiths.

These commitments, local, national, and international, have imposed the increasing necessity to raise money. At different times over the last two decades, the Temple Israel group has subscribed considerable sums to special projects. These included $50,000 for The Colman A. Zwitman Religious School Building, $37,500 for a new organ, $10,000 for The Sam C. Levenson Community House, and at present $5,000 a year for ten years toward the projected new building plans. Nor have continuing needs of the Temple been overlooked. The kitchen must be regularly refurbished and equipment replaced and added. Tables, chairs, china, glass, and silverware must be available for large and small functions in Wolfson Hall. Two thousand dollars a year is used for the receptions that follow Friday night services.

The community is larger and more affluent but not easier to reach as social relations become less personal and intimate. The annual donor luncheon continues to be the largest single money-raising event. The now regularly scheduled annual series of book reviews, "The Sound of Books," by Rabbi Narot is also a major source of income.

Sisterhood and other Temple leadership gathered at the donor luncheon, April 1972. Standing right to left: Mr. and Mrs. Martin Fine (president of the congregation and wife) and Mrs. Maurice Serotta. Seated right to left: Rabbi Nicolas Behrmann, Mrs. Howard Novell (president of the Sisterhood), Mrs. Harold Moss (chairman of the donor luncheon), Mrs. Joseph R. Narot, and Rabbi and Mrs. Barry Tabachnikoff.

Membership is encouraged but is not a major source of money. In 1946 if one partner of a newly married couple was in the family of a member, the couple received a year's membership in the congregation and the bride received a year's membership in the Sisterhood. In 1952 life membership at one hundred dollars was offered; this price was raised to $150 in 1956. Only the income from the investments of this money is used for current operations. Recently this fund has been invested in Israel bonds. Of the 670 members, nearly one fourth are life members.

The Temple Israel Sisterhood was also caught up in the soul searching that characterized the sixties. As sounds of dissidence in American society became louder, search for reasons for the dissent began. Spokesmen for institutions either became defensive or set out to discover if they were out of step with changing needs. The major questions asked had to do with the relevance of any practice or organization. The result was likely to be a reordering of priorities. Perhaps Lois Newmark, Sisterhood president in 1967, said it best in reporting to the membership on a convention:

> The contemporary woman has been released from the kitchen and has been placed in the community and has enhanced the national scene. Women are still striving for the long overdue recognition for their copartnership in all that Reform Judaism is trying to do. Women of Sisterhood can provide the moral and spiritual power that is so sorely lacking in the world today . . . our projects should reflect the needs and issues of the day. . . . Let us not be mini-mothers with mini-knowledge of how to maintain a Reform Jewish climate in our homes. . . . Sisterhood women are the bearers of Jewish values and ethics and must therefore say yes to Jewish responsibilities.

11 / Supportive Leadership

The operations of an institution as large as Temple Israel are very complex, involving many individuals and auxiliary groups as integral parts. These individuals deserve recognition; their importance is not really measured by the amount of space allotted to them in this narrative.

Assistant Rabbis

Colman A. Zwitman came to Temple Israel as an assistant rabbi in 1936 and remained to become the senior rabbi when Dr. Jacob H. Kaplan retired five years later. Assistant rabbis do not usually follow that course. It they are young men, recently ordained, as most of them are, they usually remain a few years to gain experience and then move on to congregations of their own. Even in the largest congregations they rarely remain as assistant rabbis, working in special areas without expectations of graduating to senior status.

Since 1950 the demands on the time and energy of the rabbi have become so heavy that a series of assistants to Dr. Narot have been brought to Temple Israel. Identifying them as assistants to the senior rabbi properly describes their role; they are extensions of his office. Two of them for widely different reasons deserve considerable attention. The others, including the two incumbents, have not been at the Temple long enough for us to fairly assess their talents and work.

Morris W. Graff, with the Temple from 1957 until his retirement in 1971, was unusual in that he came in his middle years and chose to remain at Temple Israel as an assistant rabbi rather than to again have a congregation of his own. He grew up in a Reform family in Cleveland, Ohio. He entered Hebrew Union College (HUC) in 1921 and worked at completing his high school studies at the same time. At HUC he received the B.A. degree with a major in history and the M.A. degree in political science; he was ordained in 1930. After seven years with a congregation in Paducah, Kentucky, he returned to HUC for a year of research with plans to study for the doctorate. He interrupted his studies to accept a post in Roanoke, Virginia, where he spent eighteen years before coming to Miami. In Paducah and Roanoke he served as president of the Public Library Board and worked with the Family Service Society at Roanoke. He was as proud of his work teaching philosophy at nearby Hollins College as Rabbi Kaplan had been of his work at the University of Miami. Graff became a recognized authority on parliamentary law, and for a time he wrote a syndicated column on the subject. He was a member of the National Association of Parliamentarians, of the American Association of University Professors, and of associations related to his religious work.

Rabbi Graff came to Temple Israel as guest rabbi, later became director of adult education, and

Rabbi Morris W. Graff

finally assistant rabbi. He had had two congregations of his own. He obviously preferred some of the activities of the office to others. At Temple Israel he and Rabbi Narot were able to work out a division of labor that served very well. Rabbi Graff preached on occasion and performed the other duties associated with the rabbi's role in the educational-religious area. He was particularly active in adult education. He took the initial steps that grew into a considerable curriculum for high school students. He liked to lecture on the roles of Biblical and historical personalities in the story of Judaism. Another specialty was his instruction of adults who wished to convert to Judaism. He was actively interested in the library, and Max Meisel, a bibliographer, worked with him in its development. The museum of Judaica, which has grown to some 200 items, was a special interest. The development of Temple archives and of oral history of the congregation were his most recent concerns. When he retired at the end of June 1971, Hebrew Union College awarded him an honorary Doctor of Divinity degree in recognition of his lifelong interest in research, learning, and teaching. He expected to continue that interest in the preparation of this history of the congregation. He died on August 15, 1971, a quietly effective man to the end of his life.

Steven B. Jacobs was a sharp contrast to Graff. He came to Temple Israel from Hebrew Union College from where he graduated and was ordained in 1967. He grew up in Boston in what he described as a very observant family in which his father in particular was Orthodox in practice. Yet the parents realized that the sons might find it necessary to live differently. The parents were willing to discuss religious questions and to leave many issues open. "It was never a matter of what one couldn't do on the Sabbath and other festivals, but what one could accomplish, given his Jewish approach," Jacobs said later. His higher education began at Yeshiva University, the Orthodox Seminary, where he was enrolled in the undergraduate program. He rebelled against the strict Orthodoxy being enforced and after two years moved to the uptown campus of New York

University where he majored in psychology and sociology. He then entered Hebrew Union College to study for the rabbinate. He departed from custom when he married in the second year of his study, and his wife completed her education at the University of Cincinnati. She was a Miami girl and Jacobs had visited her in Miami, perhaps a factor in his later coming to the city.

Jacobs interrupted his studies at HUC for one year to go to Dublin, Ireland, to help establish a congregation there. There are some 5,000 Jews in Ireland, most of them in Dublin. Some 100 families joined to establish the new Reform temple. One reason for the year abroad was the opportunity to do some soul searching, to discover if the rabbinate was the proper outlet for the objectives he had in mind for his lifework. He considered himself to be in the arena of radical Judaism. He was no less Jewish, but he was determined that something should be done to improve the lot of underprivileged people everywhere of which the Jews were but one example. He greatly admired Robert F. Kennedy and quoted him frequently, particularly a statement that expressed his view and probably accounted for his commitment to Reform Judaism. "It is an unfinished society that we offer the world—a society that is forever committed to change—to improvement and to growth that will never stagnate in the certitudes of ideology or the finalities of dogmas."

Steve Jacobs arrived at Temple Israel at the very height of the protest movement against the war in southeast Asia, and he soon became involved. He was a strong supporter of the peace movement. To the consternation of many parents who shared his idealism, he was ready to lead their children in demonstrations against what he considered injustice and immorality. He participated in the October and November 1969 moratoriums at the University of Miami. He was deeply interested in interracial problems. At Temple Israel he used a Negro convert to Judaism to help him teach a course in intergroup relations. Blacks, he said, had an identity problem as the Jews did, but blacks do not have the bootstraps on which to pull themselves up. He proposed to provide the means for them to achieve a satisfying identity and self-respect.

The widespread use of drugs by youth disturbed Rabbi Jacobs. When he spoke to a fourth-grade class at an elementary school and discovered how much they knew about the drug traffic, he wondered just how early education on the subject should begin. When the dynamic young rabbi left after three years to take a congregation of his own, as is usually the case with an effective young assistant rabbi, Dr. Narot reported that Jacobs had come to Temple Israel to gain experience and to learn to serve the congregation in the capacity of a senior rabbi. He had come particularly to respond to young people and for the young people to respond to him. Rabbi Narot described the relation as a very happy, mutual one. It should be noted, however, that the extent and diversity of the program at Temple Israel makes it possible for younger men to specialize somewhat as Rabbi Graff had done.

Assistant Rabbi Barry Tabachnikoff, who succeeded Jacobs in the position, was a classmate of Jacobs at HUC. He came with some experience since he had been assistant rabbi in Saint Louis. He is less the activist, more the serious student of Judaism. He is an accomplished musician, playing the piano, the violin, and the guitar. He performs all the functions associated with the rabbinate. Like Jacobs, he will probably get a congregation of his own rather than find a niche for himself in a large organization where the position of senior rabbi probably will not become vacant soon.

The second assistant rabbi, Nicolas Lee Behrmann, is a twenty-eight-year-old native of Philadelphia who graduated from HUC in 1971 and came to Temple Israel in July of the same year. He had some limited service in Boulder, Colorado; Norfolk, Virginia; and Morgan City, Louisiana, during his student training. He had been assistant college pastor and chaplain at Antioch College for one year. He is author of an article entitled "Multi-Media for Jewish Religious Education." He works principally with the youth groups but also assumes other rabbinical duties, including preaching.

Cantor Jacob G. Bornstein

Cantor Bornstein has been discussed in earlier chapters as a member of Rabbi Joseph R. Narot's team and as director of the religious school. In the capacity of cantor his work has been no less important. He has not been content to chant the liturgy as set forth in the Prayer Book and lead the congregation in hymn singing; rather, he has worked as imaginatively in sacred music as in religious education. He was a musician before he was a professionally trained educator. He can work in both areas only because of a rare combination of talents—a good singing voice, extensive education in Judaism, considerable administrative ability, and a deep commitment to Judaism in whatever he does.

He has been singing since he was three years old; he also recalls, "Like every good Jewish boy of my era, as a child I studied the fiddle. I studied four or five years and was pretty good at it when I was graduated from grammar school." For a time during adolescence he found other things more interesting than practicing musical instruments, but his love for singing continued. Four years in the U.S. Air Force during World War II made possible his return to school under the benefits of the GI Bill. He was enabled to take voice lessons through the help of the American Theater Wing, an agency created by the U.S. government to provide financial aid for ex-servicemen to continue their studies in art, drama, and music, subjects for which the college admission requirements for advanced study were unconventional. After a year he entered the New York branch of HUC to take a course of training leading to a degree in education and music which prepared him for the dual role he has played at Temple Israel. The study of Hebrew language, literature, and history, of the Bible and rabbinic writings, as well as of voice and instruments, makes it possible for him to work creatively in the field of sacred music. Since he has remained at

Temple Israel for two decades, one may conclude that the idea of a cantor found easy acceptance and the first cantor has been able to grow with and contribute to the rapid development of the Temple.

In an interview Bornstein explained his concept of Temple music:

> To help establish an environment, an atmosphere in which the experience of communal worship is as conducive to prayer, to meditation, to introspection as music can possibly inspire. Of course, the more beautifully rendered the music, the more effective the inspiration. The other important aspect of music in the synagogue experience of worship is the involvement of the congregation, and here I think it is becoming ever more and more evident that people prefer not to be passive in their synagogue worship. This is something I intend to engender more and more. . . . People who participate this way feel a kinship with one another.

Innovations are introduced experimentally; some survive and some do not. Bornstein is not seeking something novel to attract and entertain. His approach to music is deeply religious. The use of the harp in the chapel is an example. It is a very Jewish instrument dating back at least to the days of the Biblical David, and it adds a new dimension to already well-known music. The same may be said of the flute. The guitar has been used in some youth group meetings as an integral part of the liturgy.

Jewish music is frequently featured as it was in a festival at

Sabbath service with dance, December 6, 1968

Cantor Bornstein, at podium, practices with jazz combo for service in jazz rhythms.

the Temple in February 1962. Oratorios with Biblical themes are sometimes offered as part of a Friday evening service. In 1968 a worship service with dance was tried using rhythmic body movements to interpret the liturgy. Participants besides Rabbi Narot, Cantor Bornstein, and Temple organist, Harold Frantz, were Dean Avery, director of the Sacred Dance Guild of Miami, and some of the guild dancers. In February 1969 the rabbi and his music director tried their first jazz service. The music, composed by Charles Davison, a cantor in a northern temple, combined Dixieland jazz, southland blues, and Hebrew text and featured a five-piece jazz instrument ensemble of vibes, string bass, flute-saxophone, piano, and drums. The Temple organist conducted. College age alumni of the religious school were special guests for the occasion. In October of the same year the rabbi and the musical director presented a multimedia service using filmstrips, slides, tape recorders, and live music by guitarist Ellen Bukstel and harpist Margerita Montero in a program narrated by the rabbi. Then Rabbis Narot and Jacobs joined in preaching the sermon "Reform Judaism, Ritual, Rock and Rebellion." Special guests for the occasion were delegates to the National Association of Temple Administrators meeting in Miami. The more radical ventures are not usually repeated, but they continue to have some impact upon the concept of Temple music.

Cantor Bornstein continued his musical education and earned the Master of Music degree at the University of Miami School of Music in 1968. He has been an active member and president of the Cantors' Association of Greater Miami and has served on the Executive Board of the American Conference of Cantors. He has sung on numerous occasions for the Men's Club and other Temple groups. In February 1964 he was soloist for the Miami Beach Symphony Orchestra's presentation of Ernest Bloch's sacred service, conducted by Barnett Breeskin, in which a 150-voice interfaith choir also participated.

"Jack" Bornstein is a man of many parts, an innovative educator and cantor who willingly uses his vocal talent in congregational and community efforts and actively participates in the professional organizations for Reform Jewish religious education and music. It is not too much to say that he represents the Reform outlook at Temple Israel as widely and effectively as anyone who has been a member of the professional staff.

The Men's Club

Men have traditionally found a wide outlet for their interest in Temple affairs by service on the board of trustees. Usually, there is also a Men's Club, sometimes called the Temple Brotherhood, in each Jewish congregation as there is in many non-Jewish religious groups. Reconstructing the story of the Men's Club at Temple Israel is somewhat difficult. The Sisterhood, on the other hand, has the most complete records in the Temple archives. Minutes of all the meetings of the Sisterhood, together with well-filled scrapbooks, ensure the group of a place in history, which is always the case for those who keep records and leave them for posterity. Most of the record of the Men's Club activity is to be found in the Temple *Bulletin,* published since 1939.

Although occasional references to a men's organization appear earlier, formal organization did not occur until early 1940. The *Bulletin* for January 3, 1940, announces the birth of "a new adjunct to Temple life." Its declaration of purpose included promoting the spirit of comradeship and goodwill in the Jewish community and the spirit of friendship and helpfulness through discussions and the contributions of prominent speakers. It would "endeavor to acquaint its members with world, community and domestic affairs, and thus create a feeling of community mindedness and an atmosphere of fellowship."

For some years its role was largely educational and recreational; later, it gradually developed into something of a service agency to the congregation. Unlike in the Sisterhood, fund raising was never a major aspect of its activity. The president for the first year was B. W. Slote. The program in February of that year was typical of many to follow. Paul J. O'Connor, director of the Internal Revenue Service in Miami, spoke to the group on "Humor in Income Tax Returns." This was followed by several acts of entertainment from nightclubs of the Greater Miami area, a somewhat less common feature of programs. There was also a moonlight sailing party in May. The next season began in December with a forum at which the mayors of Miami, Miami Beach, and Coral Gables discussed municipal affairs.

In a variety of forms the forum was the common format for presenting speakers. In March of 1941 Everett R. Clinchy of the National Conference of Christians and Jews closed a five-part series. In the next year the Men's Clubs of the Unitarian Church and Temple Israel joined forces to present a series of speakers. Harry Boyell became the second president, and two new features appeared—a father-son banquet, which occasionally has become co-ed as a father-child affair, and bingo games.

During the war years the Men's Club remained inactive. Harold B. Spaet became president in 1942, and during the first year of his term the men assumed responsibility for one of the Friday evening services, including the preaching of the sermon. The *Bulletin* appeared only irregularly and in abbreviated form for two years. Spaet's name is carried through 1943 and 1944, but no activity is reported. War service was absorbing all the time and energy of the members.

In 1945 with E. Max Goldstein as president, the men's group became active again. They sponsored a Town Hall Forum at the Miami Senior High School auditorium that offered as speakers Robert St. John, Ray Josephs, Max Hill, and Erika Mann. A special feature of the regular October meeting was guest speaker Jack Bell, war correspondent and *The Miami Herald* columnist. In February of 1946 Dr. Charles H. Lee discussed "Atomic Energy for the Layman." The club was affiliated with the National Association of Temple Brotherhoods, and, after the national meeting of all UAHC groups in 1946, it sponsored a "Report to the Congregation" by delegates from the various Temple groups.

In 1947 the men of Temple Israel joined with the White Temple Methodist Church Men's Club to sponsor a Town Hall Forum that presented Pierre Van Paasen, Dorothy Thompson, John Temple Graves, and Harold Kennedy. In the following year one session featured a book review by Mrs. I. M. Weinstein. The two men's clubs also joined with the Robinson Memorial Church and the Community Church of Miami Shores to sponsor a five-lecture series opening with Dr. Gerald Wendt talking about "Atomic Energy in Peace."

In 1951 the topic of the first program was equally timely, and it might be intriguing to hear it two decades later. A panel made up of two economists from the University of Miami, John C. Fetzer and William G. Heuson, and the Hillel Director at the university, Dr. Donald Michaelson, a historian, and moderated by Ralph Renick discussed "Inflation: What Can Be Done About It." On another occasion the Men's Clubs from Temple Beth Sholem and the Coral Gables Jewish Center joined the Temple Israel meeting, and psychologist Granville C. Fisher was the speaker.

In 1952 a third type of activity begins to appear in the record. Rabbi Narot thanked the men for assuming responsibility for ushering at all Sabbath eve and Holy Days services. The men had also arranged for spot radio announcements of Temple Israel activities before and after the radio program "Message of

Israel" each Sunday. In the following year a blood bank for Temple Israel was established at Mount Sinai Hospital, and the Men's Club assumed responsibility for maintaining the supply which was available to members in any hospital in the area. In 1953 the club sponsored a series of adult education nights at which Rabbi Narot and others talked about various aspects of Reform religious practice. This activity again reflected the tendency to provide more Jewish related programs for the Temple membership rather than the secular Town Hall Forums for the general public. Recreation had by no means been forgotten. A popular duplicate bridge and canasta tournament was started in 1952 and continued for several years.

In 1957 the program included the showing of a Jewish Chautauqua Society documentary film on the High Holy Days. The Chautauqua Society, organized in 1892 to improve Jewish-Christian relations, has been a principal concern of Men's Clubs. It sends rabbis to colleges that invite them as speakers and sends books on Judaism to college libraries. Rabbi Narot has frequently been a speaker for the society. In a workshop for leaders of eight South Florida clubs early in 1958, Sylvan Lebow, executive director of the National Federation of Temple Brotherhoods, also emphasized programming and adult education. In the fall of 1963, after restudying priorities, the Temple Israel Club joined other congregational agencies in their commitment to youth activities. They proposed to provide professional and business information for Temple youth, to help to provide funds for Temple Israel Foundation for Temple Youth (TIFTY) operations, and to organize and supervise inter-Temple youth activities. The Men's Club provides financial support for its youth activities through the Morton A. Grant Fund.

In the last decade the role of the men's organization has followed a well-established pattern of activities. Their principal project involving fund raising is the Jewish Chatauqua Society. They sponsor monthly dinner meetings with a variety of speakers on contemporary subjects. Some of the dinners are open to families, and one each year is a father-son or father-child banquet. They keep up the supply in the Temple Israel blood bank and provide ushers for all regularly scheduled Temple services.

Retrospect
and Prospect

What has happened in the first half century at Temple Israel points to what may be expected in the immediate future if not for the next fifty years. Established in 1922 in an early phase of a gigantic real estate boom which collapsed in 1926, the congregation rode out a devastating hurricane in the fall of the same year. Then came the Florida depression, followed three years later by the onset of the great national depression. Before recovery was accomplished the Second World War intervened. These events reduced the first twenty-five years largely to a struggle for survival. In the second half of its first fifty years, adjustments to rapid growth and change have been equally, if not more, demanding on the congregation and its leadership.

Beyond doubt the most important decision to date is the commitment to remain in the central city. This decision means significant contribution to the revitalization of the downtown area, but it runs contrary to the nationwide flight of people and religious institutions from metropolitan areas to the suburbs. More importantly, in the case of Temple Israel it reflects the continuing determination to provide a focal point, a center, for Reform Judaism in Greater Miami. It also recognizes the obligation of the Temple to minister to the religious needs of all the loyal congregants who have moved to the surrounding communities but are loath to leave their temple.

The decision to remain in the central city imposes a heavy responsibility upon the lay and the spiritual leadership of the congregation. While they fight the declining influence of religious institutions and the decline of church attendance throughout the country, they must provide a religious and social experience that will keep people coming to 137 Northeast Nineteenth Street when often these people can affiliate with a synagogue in their own locality. The Temple must also continue to contribute to the improvement of the quality of life in the central city.

Since it has grown up with the city of Miami, the Temple has been compelled to repeatedly adjust to change in the urban environment. Flexibility must remain in the characteristic attitude toward ways and means. For example, property has been acquired for the planned expansion of the complex of facilities at the Temple site which will include a 2,000-seat sanctuary and the associated Joseph R. Narot Center for Advanced Jewish Studies. Originally projected for 1972 as a part of the golden anniversary celebration, the building program has now been given a lower priority. Membership has leveled off just short of 2,000 families, and there is no strong effort to continue expansion in size. Emphasis is upon programs.

The most obvious change of direction is toward youth-centered activities. The educational, recreational, religious, and social programs are designed to keep the youth affiliated with Reform Judaism at Temple Israel. Efforts continue to keep religion relevant in a changing social context. Jewish Reform religious and ethical ideas and ideals must be translatable into social action. There is also increased concern that the synagogue should provide for the interests and needs of members of all ages. All the activities and programs must be identified with Temple Israel and must result in pride of membership and continuing support.

Toward these goals the rabbinical staff, the cantor-educational director, the Temple administrator, and the paid professional staff work as an experienced and smooth-running team. The auxiliary organizations, particularly the Sisterhood and the Men's Club, are closely tied into a highly coordinated effort to make the Temple's program meaningful—in the words of the senior rabbi, to make it an experience rather than merely an affiliation.

Particularly among "old timers," a nostalgia remains for the good old days when the congregation was small and volunteers were the principal resources for keeping Temple services going. This feeling is, of course, characteristic of almost every phase of American life. As people move into cities in larger and larger numbers, they yearn for some aspects of the life they lived in earlier and simpler days. They cling to values inherited in an earlier day, but the mass society will increasingly modify them.

It is in this urban context that Temple Israel is committed to operate. And it may well do better than hold its own. Dynamic spiritual leadership, alert lay management, and a large congregation imbued somehow with a great sense of involvement (no small order) coupled with a flexible and imaginative program of educational, social, and religious services will be required to keep Temple Israel moving forward.

The ways in which the congregation has responded to the ups and downs of the economic cycle, to rapid growth and change, and to new moral, social, and religious concerns with a flexible and open-ended search for continuing relevance promises that the next fifty years will be equally demanding, dynamic, and successful.

Appendix A:
Presidents
of the Congregation

Term runs from May of the year indicated to May of the following year.
Presidents of the congregation are also chairmen of the board of trustees.

Harry V. Simons	1922	Jules Pearlman	1948-49
M. D. Katz	1923	Max Meisel	1950-51
Morris Plant	1924	B. W. Slote	1952
Sie Mendelson	1925	William D. Singer	1953-54
Louis Zeientz	1926	Henry E. Wolff	1955-56
Sie Mendelson	1927	Sam C. Levenson	1957-58
Day J. Apte	1928-34	A. J. Harris	1959-60
H. U. Feibelman	1935-36	Sam A. Goldstein	1961-62
Isaac Levin	1937-38	Harold Thurman	1963-64
J. Gerald Lewis	1939-40	Sam Luby, Sr.	1965-66
Frank Coret	1942-42	Elliott D. Blumenthal	1967-68
Leonard Epstein (to Dec.)	1943	Joseph Garfield	1969-70
Herman Wall (from Jan.)	1944	Martin Fine	1971-72
Max Orovitz	1944-45	Arnold Rosen	1972-73
Harold B. Spaet	1946-47		

Appendix B:
Presidents
of the Sisterhood

Term runs from May of year indicated to May of the following year.

Mrs. Max Springer (temp.)	1923	Mrs. Maxwell Hyman	1943-44
Mrs. Morris Plant	1923-24	Mrs. Leonard Epstein (Daner)	1945-46
Mrs. Max Dobrin	1925	Mrs. Isaac Levin	1947-48
Mrs. Herman Homa	1926-27	Mrs. Max Meisel	1949-50
Mrs. I. L. Seligman	1928	Mrs. Norman Giller	1951
Mrs. I. L. Rosendorf	1929-30	Mrs. Leonard Schwartz	1951-54
Mrs. Isaac Levin	1931-32	Mrs. Irving Kobley	1955-56
Mrs. I. M. Weinstein	1933-34	Mrs. Aaron Kanner	1957-58
Mrs. Isaac Levin	1935-36	Mrs. Joseph Ruffner	1959-60
Mrs. Jacob Kaplan	1937	Mrs. George Grahm	1961-62
Mrs. Milton Traverse	1938	Mrs. Joseph Bulbin	1963-64
Mrs. Harold Spaet	1939	Mrs. Morris Greene	1965-66
Mrs. Max Steuer	1940	Mrs. Clifford Newmark	1967-68
Mrs. J. Gerald Lewis	1941	Mrs. Jerome Rado	1969-70
Mrs. Harold Spaet	1942	Mrs. Howard Novell	1971-73

Appendix C:
Presidents
of the Men's Club

Term runs from May of year indicated to May of the following year.

B. W. Slote	1940	Hyman Kaplan	1954
Harry Boyell	1941	Albert J. Hirsch	1955-56
Harold B. Spaet	1942-44	Morton A. Grant	1957-58
E. Max Goldstein	1945	William Gladstone	1959-60
Louis Gillman	1946	Jesse Casselhoff	1961-62
Jerome Cohen	1947	Herbert P. Blumberg	1963-64
Henry E. Wolff	1948	Paul Barnett	1965
Michael Eisenberg	1949	Jack Schillinger	1966-67
Edward A. Klein	1950	R. Mitchell Lewis	1968-69
Herbert E. Kaufman	1951	Nat Robbins	1970-71
Jerome E. Freehling	1952	Gerald Schwartz	1972-73
Harold Friedman	1953		

Appendix D:
Charter Members

Charter approved May 31, 1923

Harry V. Simons, President
J. M. Gusky, Secretary
Morris Plant, Treasurer
Mrs. M. L. Cowen, Financial Secretary

Nathan Roth
L. Appelbaum
Leo Ackerman
Mrs. L. Axenham
H. N. Bott
Leo Bass
A. B. Cromer
M. L. Cowen
Julius Damenstein
Mrs. Carrie Miller
Chas. Peyser
M. Rubin
P. Ullendorff

B. Werner
Jack Weintraub
Rabbi Salo Stein
Max M. Nankin
R. Elfman
J. Feuer
H. Goldberg
D. Gottfried
Mrs. J. Goodman
M. Harkins
M. C. Hodes
H. H. Hyman

Dr. M. D. Katz
S. Kaufman
J. Gerald Lewis
L. Lichtensletter
S. Mendelson
B. A. Molnar
L. Stein
Joe Weiss
L. Weintraub
A. S. Zucker
Louis Wolfson
R. W. Apte

Index